TESSA& SCOTT

Our Journey from Childhood Dream to Gold

TESSA VIRTUE *and* SCOTT MOIR
As Told to STEVE MILTON

TESSA&
SCOTT

Our Journey from Childhood Dream to Gold

Foreword by TRACY WILSON

ANANSI

Hardcover edition first published in 2010 by House of Anansi Press Inc.

This edition published in 2011 by
House of Anansi Press Inc.
110 Spadina Avenue, Suite 801
Toronto, ON, M5V 2K4
Tel. 416-363-4343   Fax 416-363-1017
www.anansi.ca

Distributed in Canada by
HarperCollins Canada Ltd.
1995 Markham Road
Scarborough, ON, M1B 5M8
Toll free tel. 1-800-387-0117

Distributed in the United States by
Publishers Group West
1700 Fourth Street
Berkeley, CA 94710
Toll free tel. 1-800-788-3123

Image on page 31 (right) © James Hockings/Off Broadway Photography

15 14 13 12 11   1 2 3 4 5

Library and Archives Canada Cataloguing in Publication

Virtue, Tessa
Tessa and Scott : our journey from childhood dream to gold / Tessa Virtue
and Scott Moir ; as told to Steve Milton ; foreword by Tracy Wilson.

ISBN 978-0-88784-297-9

1. Virtue, Tessa. 2. Moir, Scott. 3. Skaters — Canada — Biography.
I. Moir, Scott II. Milton, Steve III. Title.

GV850.A2V57 2011   796.91'20922   C2011-902682-1

Library of Congress Control Number: 2011926775

Cover and book design: Gordon Sibley
Text design and typesetting: Gordon Sibley

Canada Council   Conseil des Arts   ONTARIO ARTS COUNCIL
for the Arts   du Canada   CONSEIL DES ARTS DE L'ONTARIO

*We acknowledge for their financial support of our publishing program
the Canada Council for the Arts, the Ontario Arts Council,
and the Government of Canada through the Canada Book Fund.*

Printed and bound in Canada

Mixed Sources
Product group from well-managed forests
and other controlled sources
www.fsc.org   Cert no. SW-COC-000952
©1996 Forest Stewardship Council
FSC

TESSA & SCOTT

For the seven special individuals whose names and numbers were in my BlackBerry on February 22, 2010.

—TESS
xo

For my parents, who taught me to always dream big and who gave me the opportunity to pursue those dreams.

—SCOTT

Foreword

By Tracy Wilson

I WILL NEVER FORGET THE FIRST TIME I SAW TESSA VIRTUE AND SCOTT MOIR SKATE. It was at the 2003 Canadian championships, and a friend of mine said, "You have to see this new young dance team." So, on the way to a TV production meeting I told my colleagues, "Wait, there's something I have to see." Scott was fifteen years old and Tessa was just thirteen, and they were competing in their first junior national championship. You had to stand close to the boards, because if you were too far back you couldn't see them; they were both that short. As young as they were, I immediately sensed from them an innate feeling of "dance": the musicality and rhythm they both had naturally. And each of them had what is known in figure skating as wonderful edge work: where the blade appears to take off. They were skaters; they weren't playing on the drama.

Even as junior skaters, I could see that both Tessa and Scott had that perfect balance between athlete and artist. As they matured, refined their training, and gathered more experience, that balance became even more evident.

Dance is about making it look easy, but the skill and technique has to be there first. Otherwise it's just fluff, and it shows. As an ice dancer, that's one of my biases: there's a physical, athletic side to the sport and it's absolutely essential. To me, the most important relationship in all skating is the one between the blade and the ice. And the second most important is the body to the music. If you start with these two elements, everything builds on them. That's what takes it to the next level. Jayne Torvill and Christopher Dean had it. And so do Tessa and Scott. They are pure dancers.

As a spectator, you may not understand what it is but you know that you love it. It's the pure technique, the heart of the art. That pure technique, that heart, is part of how Tessa and Scott transcend our sport more than most figure skaters ever have. Another part of transcending the sport is their universal appeal. Tessa and Scott attract everyone. An athlete can watch and appreciate the athleticism and be drawn to them. An artist can watch the beautiful shapes and be drawn to them. A musician will be drawn to them because of the sheer musicality of their work. They have something for everyone, just as Ekaterina Gordeeva and Sergei Grinkov — the greatest pairs team of our time — did.

Tessa and Scott's skating is ethereal: they take you to a higher place.

While it is Tessa and Scott who actually go out and do it, a pillar of their success is who they've found to work with over their careers. Every conceivable thing has been taken care of, every detail seen to. Marina Zoueva has the vision and wisdom to know what brilliance looks like and how to best reveal it. Igor Shpilband's technical training is, arguably, the best in the world. Marina and Igor both do choreography and technical training, but together they bring balance. And it was evident when I first saw Tessa and Scott as juniors that they had already been properly and precisely trained by, first, Carol Moir, then Paul MacIntosh and Suzanne Killing. They have such great knees, edges, and blades.

And most importantly, as people Tessa and Scott are so easy to like. They're open and they both care so much about everyone else. Watching them skate, you can see their good-to-the-bone strong character. Everything they do is for the right reasons. I went to Ilderton for their homecoming celebration, and when you see where they come from, you can understand their strength. It's based in the community and in their families. And their community becomes their family. That's their foundation, and I think it is how they were able to withstand the kind of pressure they faced in their Olympic season and with Tessa's terrible shin injuries, which were a lot worse and lasted a lot longer than anyone outside their coaches and family realized.

Much is made of Tessa and Scott becoming the first Canadians, and first North Americans, to win the Olympic ice dancing gold medal. And, it was an important milestone because in the past, political and regional biases often influenced the outcome. It was so great for the sport of ice dance to see the best team on the night win.

Their free dance will go down as one of the all-time best Olympic performances. In an often controversial judged sport such as ice dance Tessa and Scott silenced the critics, they took the sport to a new level, and one can only watch in awe and wonder at where they may take it in the future.

Tracy Wilson
Olympic Ice Dancing Bronze Medallist
Toronto, Ontario
August 2010

"I WASN'T GOOD
UNTIL I STARTED
SKATING WITH TESSA.
THE COMPETITIVENESS
REALLY PUSHED ME." —*Scott*

Chapter One

THE EARLY YEARS

DURING THEIR FIRST YEAR TOGETHER TESSA AND SCOTT FORGED WHAT WOULD BECOME AN EXTRAORDINARY ICE DANCING PARTNERSHIP.

THE FINAL JOYOUS STRAINS OF "O CANADA" still hung in the air when the roar began ripping through the arena like indoor thunder. Nearly 12,000 people, all of them on their feet, many of them still dabbing away at involuntary tears, had barely finished wailing ". . . on guard for thee!" before shifting seamlessly into yet another deafening ovation for the young woman and man on the top step of the podium.

Scott Moir pushed the flower bouquet in his left hand straight upward in celebration. Tessa Virtue hoisted the bouquet in her right. With his right hand he thrust the huge, thick gold medal away from his body toward the bellowing audience. With her left hand she subtly touched the medal dangling from her neck, almost as if she were making sure it was still there. Pure elation was written in bold letters across their faces and their bodies occasionally twitched in uncontrolled happiness. Head to toe, they visibly throbbed with joy. For the better part of an hour, bedlam and unabashed national pride had engulfed the Pacific Coliseum. The clapping and the cheering and the crying had begun partway through Tessa and Scott's brilliantly uplifting interpretation of Mahler's 5th Symphony.

It reached a crescendo as she stretched across his lap in their finishing position, his right cheek pressed against her left, their eyes squeezed shut and Scott whispering, "Thank you so much."

While they stood on the podium, after wisely letting the roars of the crowd speak alone for a few moments, veteran CTV commentator Rod Black interjected, "Only in your dreams — sometimes — does something this sweet ever happen!"

In the BBC broadcast booth, skating legend Robin Cousins told his viewers in Great Britain that the young Canadians were the only couple who could ever make him temporarily forget Jayne Torvill and Christopher Dean, fellow Britons who were considered the greatest ice dancers who ever lived.

In the vast media centre, scores of journalists hunched over their laptops hammering out their stories on deadline, trying to capture the beauty of the mood piece they had just witnessed, and recounting the seemingly mercurial rise of the youngest ice dancers, and the first from North America, ever to win the Olympics.

But only Tessa and Scott, and their families, really knew how long and difficult their journey had been, and how the most important part of it was that they had travelled it . . . together.

Opposite: Tessa Virtue and Scott Moir, gold medallists in ice dance at the Winter Olympics in Vancouver, B.C., February 2010.

TURNING NORTH OFF MIDDLESEX COUNTY Road 16 and into the Ilderton Fairgrounds, a visitor is immediately struck by two dominating images. The first is the space. The grounds, officially only 6.31 acres, spill into a horizon of rich, rolling farm fields, creating the sense of endless room. Room to breathe, room to play, and, most importantly, room to grow. The second is the big blue front wall of the Ilderton Arena and Curling Club, located only a few steps off the village's main road, directly behind the compact memorial to local war heroes. Like Vancouver's Pacific Coliseum, the site of the 2010 Olympic figure skating competition, it is the centrepiece of a vast community meeting ground, and, like the Coliseum, it is renowned for its annual exhibition and fair.

IT IS THE KIND OF PLACE WHERE YOU DON'T LOCK YOUR CAR IN THE ARENA PARKING LOT. AND IT IS THE KIND OF PLACE WHERE A BUSY LONDON FAMILY WOULD GLADLY TAKE THEIR SIX-YEAR-OLD DAUGHTER TO LEARN HOW TO FIGURE SKATE.

The Ilderton Arena, constructed in the early 1970s to replace the old Quonset hut rink, overshadows the smaller community centre, adjacent Legion Hall, and original arena, just to the west, and the exhibition hall, livestock stalls, and meticulously maintained show corrals to the north. Its outer walls — both the cinder-block lower half and the corrugated metal-siding upper half — are a distinctive and imposing dark blue, which, with its location close to the main road, makes the functional building seem bigger than it actually is.

The arena is the absolute hub of cultural life in the village. Ilderton, with three new subdivisions, has nearly doubled its population to about 2,000 residents in the last twenty-five years, but is still markedly rural. It offers the best of both worlds: the classic charm and friendliness of small-town life and the urban amenities of London, the largest city in southwest Ontario, just a ten-minute drive down County Road 20. It is the kind of place where you don't lock your car in the arena parking lot. And it is the kind of place where a busy London family would gladly take their six-year-old daughter to learn how to figure skate.

"It had such a great reputation," says Kate Virtue, whose two daughters, ten-year-old Jordan and six-year-old Tessa arrived at the Ilderton Arena in the fall of 1995. "And there was a bit of hurry to it."

Tessa's grade one class at Stoneybrook Public School in North London was scheduled for a skating outing later in the fall, and Tessa wanted to make sure she could skate well before then. "That's typical of her personality," Kate says.

Indeed, Tessa was, and still is, an extremely competitive and determined soul. She is the youngest of Kate and Jim Virtue's four children, who range widely in age. When Tessa unsuspectingly began what would be a fourteen-year odyssey to the top of the figure skating world, Kate and Jim had a child in grade one, grade five (Jordan), grade nine (Kevin), and first-year university (Casey).

Kate, a Registrar of The Law Society of Upper Canada, had studied ballet when she was young, and Jim, a lawyer, excelled at a number of sports. Their children reflected those interests and skills, engaging in a plethora of activities. Tessa began studying ballet and modern dance at Errington Graham Dance when she was three and moved to Swan Studio Dance at age six; she and Jordan also took high-level competitive gymnastics and played soccer; their older brothers played high-level hockey and football (both were quarterbacks); and Kevin was such a talented baseball player that he got a scholarship to a college in Texas and was drafted by the Baltimore Orioles. The family was busy with somebody's activities, or several of them, almost every night. Before she came to Ilderton for formal instruction, Tessa's skating experience consisted of shuffling around local London rinks "on Canadian

Above: Tessa, age 6.
Left: An early skating lesson, age 3½.
Below: The Virtue family *(left to right)* Kevin, Kate, Tessa, Jim, Jordan, and Casey.

Left: Ballet class, age 4.
Top: Tessa playing baseball, age 8.
Bottom: Tessa playing football, age 7.

Tire plastic skates" and getting rudimentary lessons from Kevin, when older brother and baby sister would grab some time together on the ice surface prior to his AAA hockey games. "As a kid I was a bruiser," Tessa recalls. "I grew up with two older brothers and an older sister, and played bodycheck hockey games and mini-sticks. When I was little, while watching my brothers play football, I was cheerleading on the sidelines, doing my gymnastics routines. I was always active. I was a bit of a tomboy. I was a tough kid."

Tumbling about with her much older siblings, trying to keep up despite their superior size and strength, helped fill the deep well of competi-

those first few days at Ilderton. "I couldn't make it around the ice. It's so funny to go back now, because it's really the tiniest little ice surface. But back then I couldn't even see over the boards. It was intimidating, because there were so many people. And I had my little helmet on." And her great big gloves on. She was small and got cold easily, so she wore huge warm mitts, prompting Danny Moir to nickname her "Big Hands."

Danny Moir and his first cousin Sheri Moir were the stars of the Ilderton Figure Skating Club. A talented team working their way up the ice dancing ladder, which in those days was a slow and very political process, they would eventually become

"AS A KID I WAS A BRUISER, I GREW UP WITH TWO OLDER BROTHERS AND AN OLDER SISTER, AND PLAYED BODYCHECK HOCKEY GAMES AND MINI-STICKS." — *Tessa*

tiveness inside of Tessa Virtue. Her mother says that she wasn't as overtly competitive as her brothers and sister, but that she "had resolve."

"I'm pretty reserved and I guess I'm shy until you get to know me. But when I get down to any activity, school too, I'm kind of a perfectionist," Tessa explains. "I see that trait in my siblings as well. And my parents are both that way, so I think it's just a part of me."

Modern dance and ballet were her first loves. But she was interested in many things, and pursued sport, piano lessons, and elementary school with the same committed drive. She always had a goal, and would pursue it relentlessly. She recalls being in the CanSkate program — a series of progressive learn-to-skate lessons administered by Skate Canada, the country's umbrella organization for figure skating — lined up in rows with her peers doing elementary exercises on one side of the Ilderton rink. But she soon noticed that the advanced class on the other side of the rink was learning far more interesting things, and was determined to get there as soon as she could. And, to one of the smallest kids on the ice, the other side was a long way away.

"Oh, it seemed huge!" she remembers of

the 1999 national novice champions and the 2001 national junior silver medallists. They trained in Kitchener-Waterloo with their coach, Paul MacIntosh, who is affectionately called "Mr. Mac," but the pair also skated regularly in Ilderton.

The Moirs were the dominant family in the Ilderton skating community. Carol and Alma MacCormack, twin sisters who moved with their army family from Ottawa to London during their teens, were good age-class figure skaters themselves and eventually became coaches. Alma travelled a four-town circuit in southern Ontario before settling into the Ilderton Club with Carol in 1983. The sisters were among the main reasons the small rink enjoyed such a big reputation and became the largest club in the London area.

Alma married Joe Moir, who grew up on the family farm on the same road as the Ilderton Arena, about four concessions to the east. Carol married Joe's older brother Paul. While Carol and Paul had three girls, Alma and Joe had three boys: Danny (born in 1980), Charlie (born in 1984), and Scott (born September 2, 1987). Scott, like his future partner, was the youngest of a rambunctious athletic bunch.

Left: Scott's baptism, October 1987.
Below: The Moir boys: *(top to bottom)* Danny, Charlie, and Scott in 1988.

Just after Danny was born, Alma and Joe Moir moved into a two-storey home on Ilderton Road, also known as County Road 16. To the south, there are expansive farm fields. A few doors to the west, more vast agricultural acreage. But along the east side of the Moir property runs a short driveway that leads directly to the Legion Hall and community centre, just a few metres behind the Moirs' backyard. About fifty metres across the parking lot looms what Scott calls "the beautiful blue" of the Ilderton Arena.

"I don't think Scott understood that not everyone grows up with an arena in their backyard," laughs Paul MacIntosh, the well-respected dance coach from Waterloo.

Because skating was front and centre in his

family, Scott doesn't really remember it not being a part of his life. Like his older brothers, he lived for hockey, and his early figure skating training was a way to improve his individual skills for the team game.

"I got put into both. My mom was a pro at the skating club, so obviously I was going to do that," he says. "If there was a CanSkate session, I might as well be on the ice trying to do it. But unlike Tessa, I had no concept of anybody getting better. When I got on, I pretty much just wanted to cause as much trouble as I could before the hour was up. I would just skate as fast as I could. I didn't care who was around me and didn't really listen to the program assistants. My mom and my aunt were in charge and I think I knew — a little bit more than they thought I did — that I could get away with a lot."

To keep home and work as separate as possible, Carol and Alma had agreed to coach each other's children. And Carol loved coaching her youngest nephew.

"For Scott and his brothers, figure skating was their second sport, hockey was the first," Carol said. "They were doing it to become better skaters for hockey. Scotty was very energetic, never standing still, and full of charisma. I could have coached him all day, he had so much energy and he made us all laugh."

Scott's ability to make people (including himself) laugh, to put them at ease, was not only important to a coach at the end of a long, tiring day, it would serve Scott well later in life when things began to get tense, as they always do at the highest levels of competitive skating.

"He's always been a little bit of a character, all three of the boys are," Alma says. "He's a good mix of our oldest two. Charlie's probably the funniest but also the quietest. Danny is easy to get to know. We always got compliments on how he talked to adults. He was always out there, while Charlie was a bit more reserved. Scott's the youngest, so maybe he needed to show off to get attention. We don't have pictures of him being serious; he always has a great smile on his face."

Scott took his earliest figure skating lessons in hockey skates, as many of the boys in Ilderton did.

Clockwise:
Joe and Scott,
summer 1988;
Scott in "Country
Bear Jambouree,"
age 4; Scott's
kindergarten
photo, 1992–93;
Danny, Charlie,
and Scott, 1990.
Centre: Scott,
18 months.

But when he was six and starting to learn elementary toe jumps, he needed figure skates with their toe picks. He got two pairs of hand-me-downs from one of his cousins, but they were white. One pair the family painted black, and the other required black boot covers to hide the original colour.

"One time, my mom had forgotten to put one boot cover on," he says. "I can remember one of the rink guys saying 'nice white skates' so I wouldn't go on the ice. I had one white skate, and one black skate, and I thought the world was going to figure out that the black skate was actually a white skate too. White skates were supposed to be for girls."

At the time, Scott was playing a great deal of hockey for Ilderton teams, one year in a more local league against other teams from small towns, the next in AAA, the highest level in Ontario minor hockey. He admits that he far preferred hockey to skating — he played at a high level until his early teens — and would often cry and hide in his room when his father said it was time to make the short walk to the arena for figure skating practice. Once he got to the rink, however, he was enthusiastic.

"I never compared the two sports when I was young, they were completely different," he says. "The figure skating always made my hockey better, but when I played hockey and came back to figure skating it just made it a lot worse. I would bend over again and I would hit my toe picks a couple of times. My buddies always said that when I played hockey they could tell I was a figure skater, because I had a good back and good posture."

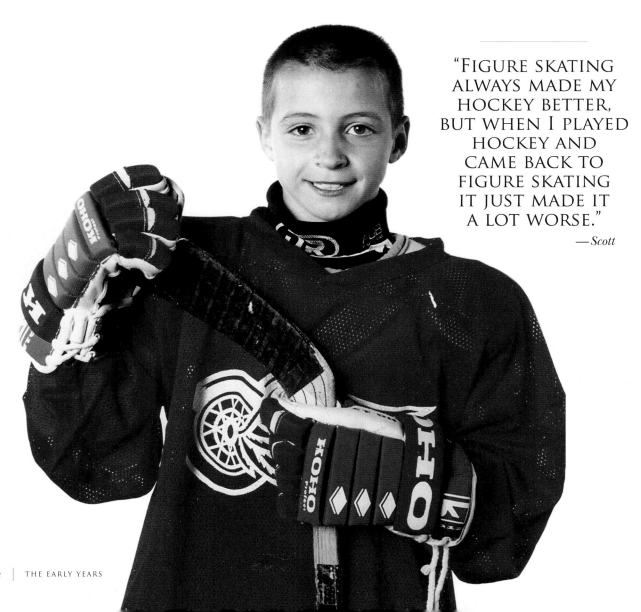

"FIGURE SKATING ALWAYS MADE MY HOCKEY BETTER, BUT WHEN I PLAYED HOCKEY AND CAME BACK TO FIGURE SKATING IT JUST MADE IT A LOT WORSE."

—*Scott*

When Tessa started skating in Ilderton, Scott had just turned eight, had already done his first solo, *Sesame Street Rock*, and had taken a liking to the jumps. To lighten the load on a very active family with two working parents, Kate Virtue's mother, Eleanor, often drove Tessa the fifteen or twenty minutes from the Virtue family home near the University of Western Ontario to Ilderton once or twice a week for her skating lessons. One incident from that first winter not only rings with irony, given where Tessa eventually went with skating, it hints at the source of Tessa's lifelong love of fashion.

"Scott's aunt, Carol, was my singles coach," Tessa says, "and one day she said, 'We're going to sign her up for Test Day,'" [a day when skaters are evaluated against Skate Canada standards] "but my grandma said, 'No, no, no, we're not taking this seriously. No tests, no competitions, this is just for fun,' because I was doing so many other sports, was serious about gymnastics and was very competitive. Then my mom heard that Test Day might be an opportunity to buy a dress, so she signed me up."

While Tessa and Scott were nearly oblivious to each other's presence over Tessa's first two winters at the rink, their mothers weren't.

"I do remember seeing Scott," Kate Virtue says. "He was dancing with another little girl at the time. You could pick the Moir kids out by the way they skated. They were the best in the rink. He was adorable and he had kind of an impishness to him."

And Alma Moir had noticed Tessa: "She always wore these big mitts. And she had the gymnastic body, the dance training, and the dancer's back."

Carol Moir, who was teaching both of them singles skating, says Tessa was "a very petite athlete. Freckle-faced and pigtailed. Very cute. She was very small but very athletic. And she was always very mature for her age. She was athletically developed so I always had to remind myself, 'this girl is only seven years old.'"

Neither Scott nor Tessa remembers the specific moment they met, comparing it to school where "you just sort of realize you know somebody," but they do remember becoming much more familiar with each other during the summer camps at the arena.

Opposite: Scott's hockey photo from Mid-Elgin Red Wings team.
Above right: Tessa with her grandmother Eleanor.
Above left: Skating carnival, March 1996.
Right: Tessa at age 7.

"He had a buzzed head," Tessa says.

"It was summer, man, it was a buzz cut," Scott replies.

"Sometimes you'd dye it blond."

"Yeah, I did a whole bunch of things to it."

The camp, which provided an all-day program of swimming, crafts, gym, ballet, karate, and figure skating, was called MAC, an acronym for Marg, Alma, and Carol, the three coaching sisters. Later, they realized that MAC was also the nickname of their father, Irven MacCormack.

"We were in all the same classes together," Scott continues. "I was getting kicked out of the ballet classes, because I was just goofing around. We were by far the youngest in our group. We were pretty good, and everybody else was probably in seventh or eighth grade."

Tessa says of those first two summers, "I don't remember necessarily a first attraction but I remember always sort of being aware of where Scott

Left: (left to right)
Scott, Charlie, Danny,
Sheri Moir (cousin),
Tessa, Leanne Moir
(cousin), and Jordan.
Below: (top to bottom)
Danny, Charlie,
and Scott, skating
carnival 1998.

was in the rink. He never stayed in one spot. In any activity group he was kind of buzzing about, but I was always keeping an eye on him for some reason."

Generally, though, like most kids of that age, skaters at the camp were less interested in what individuals were doing than what groups were up to, particularly the pranks.

"One time the girls took all the boys' skating clothes and replaced them with spandex skirts," Tessa laughs. "And the guys wore them on the ice."

The boys came up with a plan to pay the girls back, but it didn't have quite the intended result.

"We wanted to put chickens in their dressing room," Scott says. "But we couldn't get any chickens at that time of year, so we got little chicks instead and the girls all went 'Awwww, they're so cute!' They wanted to take them home."

Among the other campers were Scott's brother Charlie, his cousins, and Tessa's older sister, Jordan.

"My brother would constantly play tricks on me," Scott says, with great respect for Charlie's creativity. "He'd say, 'Let's play hide-and-seek, because we don't want to go to dance class.' So I'd walk into the dance class forty minutes late because I'd been hiding in the closet. And my brother had been sitting there the whole time."

Foreshadowing a deeper relationship between the families, the Moir and Virtue kids all got along, and Cara Moir and Jordan Virtue became good friends. In fact, they played a major, if unforeseen, role in creating one of the greatest partnerships in Canadian skating history.

"My sister and Scott's cousin decided it would be kind of cute if we were 'dating,'" Tessa says. "And I liked Scott. I don't know if he liked me, but we just went along with it."

"Were we not the hot topic by week four, though?" Scott asks rhetorically. "We were the big new couple on campus. We 'dated' for eight months. Why do I remember that? Because eight months is a long time for eight and ten years old. We probably only had two phone conversations and I remember my brothers talking me through the phone call with her, I was so nervous. We'd sit there and not say anything. It was a cool thing to do: phone and talk to each other."

"MY SISTER AND SCOTT'S COUSIN DECIDED IT WOULD BE KIND OF CUTE IF WE WERE 'DATING,' AND I LIKED SCOTT. I DON'T KNOW IF HE LIKED ME, BUT WE JUST WENT ALONG WITH IT." — *Tessa*

"Dating" was a little strong. It was the summer of 1997, and heading into grades three and five they were too young for even puppy love, so it was just a label that others attached to them, mostly for their own amusement.

Tessa talked about Scott during school hours at Stoneybrook Public School, but when Scott's friends at Oxbow Public School found out about Tessa, he somehow felt he had to "end" it. His friends called Tessa and quickly handed the phone back to Scott, who blurted, "I don't want to go out with you any more," then hung up.

And although for the next dozen years every reporter and skating fan, and eventually, millions of TV viewers, tried to link them as boyfriend and girlfriend, that has been the extent of their romantic history.

"But, after we got over our little relationship thing, we were actually able to talk more," Scott says. "And our relationship grew."

Tessa always wondered whether Jordan and Cara talking about her and Scott "dating" had any influence on Cara's mother pairing the two together.

"They have to take the blame, or I guess I should say the credit," Carol Moir says. "Scott had a former dance partner, for two months leading to a local competition the previous winter, and she had decided she didn't want to do it any more. That fall I was thinking, 'I've got to find Scott another partner.' And then Tessa skated by. Cara and Jordan had already put them together and Tessa was the right size and the proper skill level for Scott. And the families got along well, and that's very important in partnerships."

Tessa had only just started grade three but says, "one thing I do remember vividly was Carol calling me over — Scott was standing with her — and just getting me to stand beside Scott to see height-wise how we matched. I remember standing there and not knowing what she had in mind and not even thinking this would be a partnership

Tessa and Scott, 1998.

thing. I just remember thinking, 'Why are we comparing heights here?' It was in front of the window in the corner. I can picture it so vividly. Then she had us skate perimeter, where you just skate left-right-left-right."

"We did not get it the first time," Scott says, picking up the story. "We kept hitting each other in the perimeter. Then we did a couple of exercises in the dance position, and that was a lot of work for the first day. I think I was thinking, 'When can I go and skate by myself?' You're so shy at that age. I remember being so nervous holding her hand, even though she had these huge mitts on. I was just so nervous, we were probably barely touching each other. I just wanted it to be over."

Neither the eight-year-old nor the ten-year-old had any clue from that first shaky foray that they were headed for a full-time partnership. In fact Tessa, who had been partnered for a few instructional dances with Scott's older brother, had written in her grade one notebook that her dream was to go to the Olympics "with DANNY Moir."

Above: With coach
Carol Moir in 1998.
Left: Tessa solo, 1997.

Both Tessa and Scott demonstrated skating skills beyond their years and each reached the Western Ontario sectionals (the first of two steps toward the national championships) in singles, which is an accomplishment given the number of skaters in the region.

Tessa was the first and only skater Carol Moir ever taught who mastered a single Axel in one lesson. She loved to skate fast, and loved doing spiral after spiral in front of the arena window. "And I suppose that even at that age I was kind of a performer," she says. According to those closest to her, whenever she skated, even at the youngest age and perhaps from her dance training, she had the poise and projection to capture every pair of eyes in the arena.

"I loved doing double jumps, but when it came to starting a double Axel or a triple jump, I didn't really want to do it," Tessa says. "I wasn't scared. I just liked landing things. As I said, I'm a perfectionist."

Because they had always been the smallest and youngest, growing up with older siblings, taking classes with older skaters, playing hockey or competing in gymnastics against older athletes, and having friends who were older, Tessa and Scott were always trying to keep up. So at the time Tessa hadn't realized she had become a very good skater, Scott hadn't realized he had become a very good skater, and neither knew that they were already showing a germ of promise as a dance couple. Carol had talked to both sets of parents about it, and Tessa and Scott were soon skating almost exclusively with each other during dance sessions, thereby forming an unspoken partnership.

"We were so young that we just kept doing what we were told," Scott recalls. "I wasn't good until I started skating with Tessa. As she says, the competitiveness really pushed me. Before, I didn't care. Once I was skating with Tessa, she would do something and I would say to myself, 'I guess I'd better learn how to do that better than her or else it's going to look like this girl's beating me.' That was a lot of what motivated me."

"And in our singles, when we weren't skating together," Tessa continues, "it was, 'Oh, he's doing his double toe. I'm going to do MY double toe.'"

Even at their first summer camp together they were competitive at the ping-pong table. (A memory that would come back to Scott more than a dozen years later, watching Sidney Crosby and his teammates wage spirited table tennis tournaments in the Olympic Village. Tessa wasn't able to spend a lot of time in the athlete's lounge because of

> "I LOVED DOING DOUBLE JUMPS, BUT WHEN IT CAME TO STARTING A DOUBLE AXEL OR A TRIPLE JUMP, I DIDN'T REALLY WANT TO DO IT, I WASN'T SCARED. I JUST LIKED LANDING THINGS. AS I SAID, I'M A PERFECTIONIST." — *Tessa*

extensive physiotherapy sessions, but she recalls that they also played a lot of bubble hockey in her basement when they were kids. Tessa points out that she can still beat Scott when they play on the bubble hockey game at the rink when they need a diversion from training. To which Scott jokingly replies, "Tessa is stretching this, she can't beat me at bubble hockey.")

That doubly fuelled competitiveness was tempered nicely by the attitude that the Moirs in general, and Scott in particular, brought to the sport. They were expected to practise diligently, and compete to the best of their ability. "But we always had fun with it too," Scott explains. "We were always a pretty easygoing family, and we knew it wasn't really that important to win the home-region championships. So if something went wrong, we just kind of laughed it off. And we always made jokes at each other. There were always six of us there competing. Six Moirs. We knew if you had a really bad program, you could always look up in the stands and they'd all be there laughing at you anyways."

Tessa remembers watching Scott in a local singles competition when he was about ten years old. "He was about to skate to his "Lone Ranger" program and was nervous about going on. His cousin

"I WAS TEN YEARS OLD, I DIDN'T HAVE
THE ALLOWANCE TO BUY FLOWERS.
I KISSED HER ON THE CHEEK THAT NIGHT
TOO. SHE HAD TO BE IN THE NEXT NUMBER
RIGHT AWAY SO IT PROBABLY WASN'T
THE BEST TIME." — *Scott*

Leanne, I think trying to relax him, said, 'Okay, Scott, do a back flip. He was doing a backwards shoot-the-duck and was supposed to get up and go into a single Lutz jump. But instead he did a back roll on the ice and just kept going. His face did not change a bit. He was straight-faced, and looked almost disinterested. I remember vividly, sitting in the stands with his mom, and she was laughing!"

It was clear to the grown-ups around them that through these shared experiences, their rapidly escalating skating skills, and their innate matched competitiveness, Tessa and Scott were becoming uncommonly close friends, even if they couldn't recognize it themselves.

PAUL MACINTOSH WAS VISITING ILDERTON once a week to coach Danny and Sheri Moir, his rising ice dance team, and it was natural that he would watch another Moir and his new partner and sometimes work with them. He recalls seeing Tessa and Scott in the first year of their partnership. "Scott likes to play down the relationship they had when they were young, but even as young people they seemed to beat with one heart," Paul says. "They had an uncanny sense of unison. And there was a sense of something in their ankles and knees that told you they had musicality and a sense of rhythm. Once in a lifetime you get kids like that."

What Scott saw as "doing what we were told" his coaches saw as one of the most important assets in individual sport: coachability. Carol Moir identified it in both kids right away, and all the coaches they would encounter in the future would be grateful for the young team's willingness to quickly grasp instructions and then follow them, no matter what they might have thought about those instructions.

While much of that was native to their individual personalities, some of it was clearly born in the safety and comfort of an arena where maximum effort was expected but where it was okay, and sometimes worth laughing about, to make an honest mistake. And where the coaches enjoyed your complete trust because not only were they skilled and perceptive, they were friends and family.

Tessa and Scott's partnership through most of that initial year together (and Tessa's second winter at the rink) consisted mainly of skating together to the four dances that would be played on the arena sound system during group training sessions.

"I knew we were kind of partners," Scott recalls. "When Tessa was on the ice I'd think 'Oh, we're going to have to skate together today.' That kind of thing. It was sorta cool, but very nerve-racking to be skating with a girl and holding hands. I liked Tessa. But I was just kind of cruising around. I still really wanted to be a singles skater. It just happened one day that we were together."

By the time the Ilderton Skating Carnival, the highlight of the local skating calendar, rolled round in April 1998, Tessa and Scott were in a loosely knit partnership. But during the carnival they performed only as singles skaters. It was during their "dating" phase, and both were portraying acrobats, once again triggering the mutual competitiveness that fuelled their skating.

"You gave me flowers," says Tessa, giggling. "But I was going to get them anyways. You just happened to grab them from the bucket and give them to me."

"I was ten years old," Scott retorts. "I didn't have the allowance to buy flowers. I kissed her on the cheek that night too. She had to be in the next number right away so it probably wasn't the best time."

W.O.S. Fall Invitational

1998

Tessa & Scott

Opposite: Presenting flowers at Ilderton Carnival, 1998.
Above: A Polaroid from the Western Ontario Section Invitational.
Right: Tessa and Scott, 1999. *Below:* Scott's grade school photo.

Tessa
here is my
picture.

To The
Best Partner
EVER, Love Scott

That winter, Carol Moir suggested to Tessa and Scott that they enter a Western Ontario Section invitational event where they would be required to perform a swing dance. "In order to motivate us to actually work, you throw a competition in there, or a test," Scott theorizes, but this particular duo needed far less motivation to work than anyone their age, or much older.

At the event, both sets of parents were standing together on the wooden steps of the arena, laughing because their children "looked so cute" together, Kate Virtue recalls. "But we couldn't let the kids see us laughing. Tessa was wearing one of Sheri's skating dresses which was missing a few beads, which bothered Tessa. Then Alma said, laughing. 'Oh, he's doing the wrong steps!' Scott had forgotten his steps."

Nobody can remember where they finished in that event, but what emerged from their debut competition together was perhaps the first

ritual, and certainly an early pillar, of their relationship. From that point on, Tessa always learned both her own and Scott's steps for every competitive program. "He's always forgotten his," Tessa says. "From the beginning I learned that if I made a mental note of his steps, then I'd be able to help him a little bit." It was an early signpost of the give-and-take required to sustain a long-term partnership, although neither was thinking of it that way at the time.

During the spring skating school after the 1998 carnival, Tessa and Scott found themselves training more and more often together, and there was a formal acknowledgement of their partnership. Joe, Alma, and Scott Moir and Jim, Kate, and Tessa Virtue began what would become their annual spring meeting to make sure the kids wanted to commit to another season of lessons and training. By mutual agreement, it was to be a year-to-year process.

"With Tessa and Scott, we'd take it one year at time," Carol Moir adds. "If Tessa took after her dad and grew tall and Scott didn't, they'd both have to move on to other partners."

While Tessa did have a growth spurt and Scott's came later on, through most of their career they have been close to the same height. It's one of the traits that skating people always notice when seeing them for the first time.

As the 1997–98 season drew to a close, Carol Moir considered it a "really fun first year together." Tessa and Scott had evolved, rather than jumped, into an ice dance partnership. "It was never a conscious decision for either of us to say, 'Okay, I'm going to go the dance route,'" Tessa says. "Or even 'I want to be a figure skater.' I never said that, or really had a chance to decide that. It just kept going."

"I always think that dance kind of chose us," Scott continues. "There's no doubt that we enjoyed doing it. We were pretty young, but we always had a lot of fun with it. It was kind of exciting, and the ball just never stopped rolling."

But wider input would be needed to keep that ball rolling. They might have arrived at ice dancing almost accidentally, but underneath Scott's serial playfulness and Tessa's outsized sophistication they were both unusually determined and competitive kids and were already thinking about becoming the best they could be, probably with the Olympics swimming subconsciously around in their minds. And no matter how well Carol Moir had constructed those first physical and psychological steps, for Tessa and Scott to climb the ice dance ladder — the most hierarchical in all of figure skating — their coach knew they would eventually have to look beyond the big beautiful blue of Ilderton.

"I ALWAYS THINK THAT DANCE KIND OF CHOSE US."

—*Scott*

Opposite and Above:
Tessa and Scott
during the first year
of their partnership.

"THEY HAD A
MUSICALITY
THAT WAS DIFFERENT
THAN ANY OTHER KIDS
I HAD EVER TAUGHT.
IT WASN'T JUST THE
(TIME) COUNT,
IT WAS THE CHARACTER
AND THE WAY THEY
PLAYED OFF
EACH OTHER." —*Suzanne Killing-Wood*

Chapter Two

COMPETITIVE EDGE

AN UNEXPECTED CHAMPIONSHIP WIN PROMPTED THE FIRST INKLING THAT SOMETHING SPECIAL WAS ON THE HORIZON FOR TESSA AND SCOTT.

"IT WAS A NATURAL," CAROL MOIR SAYS, THAT Tessa and Scott should start gradually working with Paul MacIntosh, who had taught all levels of skating and was respected for elevating promising skaters into international athletes. "Mr. Mac" was already coaching Scott's oldest brother, Danny, and Carol's middle daughter, Sheri, in Kitchener-Waterloo, where, Carol says, "They had ice five days a week, and in our little arena we got only three days of skating a week."

So, in the summer of 1998, less than a year after they had stood side-by-side comparing heights in front of the window in the Ilderton Arena, Tessa and Scott began travelling the 100 kilometres to Kitchener once a week to take lessons from Paul and his young assistant Suzanne Killing. They continued those trips, once or twice per week, through the school year — Tessa was in grade four at Stoneybrook Public School in London, Scott in grade six at Oxbow Public School in Ilderton — and as they became more and more immersed in ice dance and their partnership, they steadily increased the frequency. By the 1999–2000 season they were making the hour-long commute three or four, and sometimes five, mornings a week, and they soon began devoting parts of their summers to living and training in Waterloo. Carol continued to teach them their singles lessons and, in regular communication with Mr. Mac, would assist with

Opposite: At Tomorrow's Champions Competition, 2000. *Above:* Tessa and Scott at a training session during the 1999–2000 season.

their dance steps and programs whenever they were on the ice at Ilderton Arena.

"We would meet at 4:45 or 5 a.m. at the Bethel Church on Ilderton Road," Tessa recalls. "That church was a big part of our childhood because that's where we'd spend so much time waiting for each other. We'd switch cars to whichever parent was driving us that day. Then we'd fall asleep right away. And we'd wake up just before we got to the rink. Then, after we skated, we'd get a hot chocolate, drive back, and change cars again at Bethel Church or we'd be dropped off at school."

That was a time and energy expenditure far beyond what other children their age could conceive of, but Tessa and Scott had already become dedicated to their sport and to each other. And in that summer of 1998, Tessa dramatically put words and action to that commitment.

To this day, despite how much Tessa loves skating, ballet and modern dance — "dance, period" — are still her deepest passions. "I was always choreographing dances off the ice, even hip-hop," she says. She continued to take ballet lessons from Jennifer Swan in London and was part of a London company called Children's Dance Project, performing recitals around the city. Later, she went to classes at Kitchener's Carousel Dance Studios two or three times a week.

Tessa cut skating camp short in the summer of 1998, because she had auditioned for the National Ballet School in Toronto and wanted to spend July in the school's summer program. It was an incredibly intense month and for the first two weeks, the students were not allowed to have any contact with friends or family.

Opposite: Tessa and Scott during the 1999–2000 season.
Above: At the rink in Kitchener, Ontario. *Below*: An informal practice session.

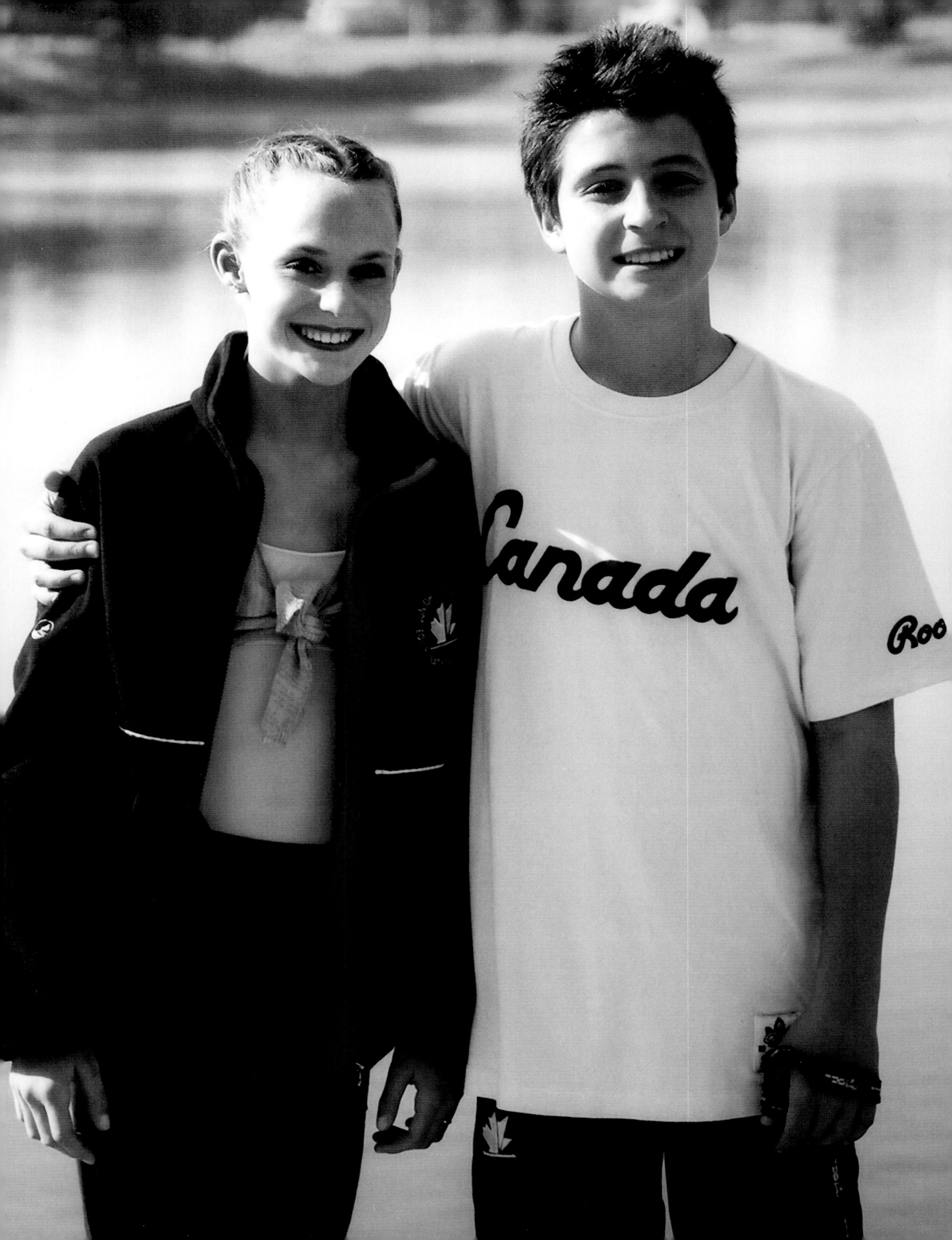

Canada
Roo

"It was stressful," Kate Virtue recalls. "When Tessa was finally allowed to call home she was crying. But she said, 'I'm not crying because I'm sad, I'm crying because I'm so happy to talk to you.'"

Kate, with her own history in ballet, confesses she secretly hoped that her daughter would choose to attend the National Ballet School, but she left that decision to Tessa. And Tessa, reasoning it out herself, turned down the institution that so many other girls her age were dying to attend.

"A big part of me wanted me to do it and if I hadn't been skating with Scott, that's what I would have done," she explains. "I'd already committed to Scott. Our parents didn't ever put pres-

ton. Tessie was that little girl who looked adults right in the eye when she talked to them. She was, and is, open and gregarious but not in a way of grandstanding or showing off. She's imbued with a work ethic, but I don't think she sees it as work. She's excited to get up at 6 a.m. and work for something. She'd watch Jordan's class and afterward she could do, without having tried it, what some of the senior girls at her sister's level were having trouble grasping. So she takes a lot of joy in trying things. Is it hard? Yes it is, but it doesn't scare her. I really think she believes she's dancing when she's skating. It's very soulful. There is an honesty: Tessa believes in every moment she creates, and if she

"'THIS IS THE FIRST TIME A NINE-YEAR-OLD HAS TURNED DOWN THE NATIONAL BALLET SCHOOL BECAUSE SHE HAS A PARTNER!'"

— *Mavis Staines, Artistic Director, National Ballet School*

sure on us, but if we committed to the season at those yearly meetings we were going to finish the season. And I knew that if I skated, I could still do ballet as a hobby, but that if I went to the National Ballet School there was no way I could continue skating."

"It was a huge decision," Kate recalls. "When she told the school no, that she was committed to her skating partner, Mavis Staines, the artistic director, said, 'This is the first time a nine-year-old has turned down the National Ballet School because she has a partner!'"

The school clearly wanted Tessa to enroll and Mavis Staines telephoned her dance teacher Jennifer Swan in London to find out if there was anything she could do.

"Typically people are chomping at the bit to get into the school," Jennifer recalls. "She really did stand out within our students. But Tessa and her family had already had a lot of reinforcement about skating. The skating world was indicating that they could go places. Tessa is a very loyal person and that commitment she has to her partner and her work is part of her stage presence."

Jennifer continues, "She was cute as a but-

doesn't she challenges it. She and Scott are both that way with the people they work with."

Tessa auditioned again the following summer, but made the same decision for the same reason, and Kate knew that her daughter would not attend the National Ballet School, although at the yearly spring meetings between the Moirs and Virtues, she kept expecting Tessa to say she wasn't going to maintain the heavy skating commitment because of her other interests. But she never did.

Meanwhile, Scott was demonstrating his faith in the partnership in a different way. Sensitive, emotional, and caring for a boy of his age, Scott took an early liking to ice dancing because of its speed, precision, and intricacy. But he was discovering that he really only liked ice dancing with Tessa Virtue. Paul MacIntosh would have his dance students do "circuits" in which they'd skate a lap with their regular partner, then switch to do a lap with someone else's partner. As he grew older, Scott would also partner other dancers through the various levels of testing. In either situation, his inner reaction was the same. "Every time, I'd say to myself, 'Okay Tessa, come back.' I hated to skate with anyone else but Tess.

Above: At competition with coaches Suzanne Killing and Paul MacIntosh. *Below:* On the ice before competition in 2000.

Those poor girls. I was probably pretty rough on them, because they weren't as good as Tessa and they wouldn't hold themselves as well as Tessa did. And that really frustrated me."

Native ability, Carol Moir's early instruction, and healthy competition between the two youngsters gave Tessa and Scott a solid grounding in core skating skills. They were both fast, had good balance and posture, and were keenly aware of the proper use of edges, so necessary to maintain power and flow and for presenting a unified look below the knees. But when they started working with Paul, "that was when we really built our foundation, that's for sure," Tessa says. "Paul had us doing a ton of stroking and was really breaking it down into the basics of skating."

Paul had taught Suzanne Killing (now Suzanne Killing-Wood) and Peter MacDonald when they were nationally ranked junior ice dancers in the early 1990s. And when Suzanne retired at the age of seventeen, Paul convinced her to pursue her Skate Canada coaching certification. She had been one of the most creative students he'd ever had and had an innate understanding of music and its application to skating. When Tessa and Scott began making their pre-dawn treks from Bethel Church, Suzanne was twenty-three and she and Paul were working together at several different rinks in Kitchener and Waterloo.

"They were eight and ten when they came to Waterloo," recalls Suzanne. Her first impression of Tessa and Scott was that "they were a little vision. There was already talk about them. I knew of Scott and I was anticipating the third Moir anyway.

"They had a musicality that was different than any other kids I had ever taught. Whether in simple dances or more complex ones, you could see the music was fuller to them more than to the other kids. It wasn't just the (time) count, it was the character and the way they played off each other. Usually at that age you have to get the kids to count out loud to the music — 1-2-3-4 — but I never had to do that with Tessa and Scott. And Tessa, of course, would add her flair."

The young team were still getting most of their ice time in Ilderton and were preparing for the Western Ontario sectionals in the juvenile category, but in late autumn of 1998, just a week before sectionals, Scott broke his right arm playing flag football. (In later years, when Scott was trying to recall the incident, Tessa would

have to remind him which arm he had broken.) "My doctor said to me, 'I'm going to put you in a cast, and you *could* go skating, but this is the arm you have to use for the rest of your life.' My grandfather was with me and he told my parents, 'No way, I was there talking to the doctor, he can't go.' So we had to skip sectionals and decided to go to the all-Ontarios, which is what you do when you can't go to sectionals and then Nationals. We went there and we won that."

"In the scheme of things, it's not that big, but it was big to us at the time," Tessa recalls.

The provincials, held in Woodstock, Ontario, in January 1999, was their first formal victory, and as all competitions would continue to do for the duration of their careers, it whetted their appetite for more.

Scott *didn't* break his arm the following season, and the increased training in Waterloo paid off in a victory at the juvenile sectionals, earning them a berth in Tomorrow's Champions, a prophetic title for the national pre-novice and juvenile championships. The following year, novices would also be added to Tomorrow's Champions, as

Skate Canada tried to get its younger stars more attention rather than having them be overshadowed by the juniors and seniors at the regular Canadian Championships.

Both skaters were excited to make their first major trip, to Kelowna, British Columbia, and to get their Western Ontario team jackets. Tessa confesses that one of her main goals as a six-year-old starting her first group classes in Ilderton had been to become good enough to earn one of the jackets, with "Program Assistant" emblazoned on

> "WE WERE IN IT FOR ALL THE PERKS. WE WANTED TO SEE KELOWNA, WANTED TO WEAR OUR JACKETS, WANTED TO BE PART OF THE TEAM. IT WAS SO EXCITING, THE WHOLE EXPERIENCE. BUT WHEN WE GOT OUT ON THE ICE I WAS SO NERVOUS. —*Scott*

the back, that were given to helpers in the CanSkate program. Now she had a more important jacket of her own.

"That was our breakthrough," Scott said of qualifying for Tomorrow's Champions. "We were scared, though. The size thing was a huge factor for us. And we'd never been in a national competition before, so we had no idea how we'd place."

"And it was a big rink with lights and judging stands," Tessa adds.

"We were usually in such c-o-o-o-l-l-l-ld arenas, and Tess would be shaking; a dark, hometown hockey rink," Scott continues. "We were in it for all the perks. We wanted to see Kelowna, wanted to wear our jackets, wanted to be part of the team. It was so exciting, the whole experience. But when we got out on the ice I was so nervous. Scared. I can remember looking up in the stands and Paul was talking to us and I wasn't listening at all. He was saying, 'Hel-lo, you're at the national championships!'"

In order to foster proper grounding in the sport, juvenile and pre-novice championships are made up of two compulsory dances and a

Top: Informal practice.
Above: With Paul at Tomorrow's
Champions competition.
Right: Posing for photos after gold medal
win at Tomorrow's Champions competition, 2000.
Opposite: With Suzanne Killing after a win at
Juvenile Sectionals, 1999.

Above: (left to right) Alma, Tessa, Scott, Carol, and Kate
after gold medal win.
Right: In Kelowna, B.C., March 2000.
Opposite: On the ice during a competition.

"combination" free skate. In that limited free skate,
couples must skate a pattern of a prescribed dance
— in Kelowna that year it was the Ten-Fox — and
then proceed to steps of their own creation. Tessa
and Scott weren't expecting to win, nor were they
expected by insiders to win. But at the end of the
compulsory dances, they stood first.

"We were thinking, 'Oh, wow, we've got a
chance to win this,'" Scott says. "But then we went
back to our parents to say how cool that is, they
said 'Well, yeah, it is cool but it doesn't really matter where you come, it's just about skating well and
having fun.' We went out there and said, 'Let's do
this thing,' and we ended up winning. We were the
youngest team in the championship, and on the
podium we were the shortest. I remember standing
with my hands stretched in the air so I could put
them around the shoulders of the other couples.
We were juvenile national champions and even
though it didn't really mean that much, I was
thinking, 'Oh, wow, I really like this competing
thing. I really like competitive ice dancing, and we

can really do something with this. NOW I want to
win pre-novice.'"

"I didn't have the same realization as Scott,
not at that point," Tessa says. "I had fun in Kelowna
and I met a lot of people. But in those early years,
the absolute best part of any of it for me was the
choreography. It was so much fun and I just lived
for that."

The unexpected championship in Kelowna
was a watershed moment for the young couple. It
was then that those closest to them had their first
inkling that something special might be percolat-
ing for Tessa and Scott. When the event opened,
Kate Virtue, who was new to this level of skating
competition, had found herself hoping only that
they wouldn't finish dead last. But she was assured
by Alma Moir, as she watched group after group,
that their children weren't going to be "last or even
second last. They're as good as this group." Carol
Moir recalls thinking, "Wow, they're either really
very good or everyone else is very bad." And she
didn't believe it was the latter. Alma Moir knew

"THEY WERE SO LITTLE AND SO YOUNG,
BUT MOSTLY LITTLE, BUT THEY SKATED BIG." —*Alma Moir*

they were good, but as a veteran of skating she also knew that judges can have their own priorities and preconceptions, especially in ice dancing. "They were so little and so young, but mostly little," Alma says. "But they skated big." Suzanne and Paul were surprised at how far their team, and it was now *their* team, had come in such a short time. Paul told "Skate Canada officials and anyone who would listen, 'You're never going to see a rise in a dance team like this one."

In their first exposure to the country's best young talent, Tessa and Scott were also studying how to act like a dance team. They watched the pre-novices and imitated them in terms of warming up, how to bow to the audience, even how to get onto the ice from the other side of the boards.

Tessa and Scott continued to train individually in singles with Carol, and she told both of them that had they not succeeded in ice dancing, they would have been excellent free skaters.

Above: Suzanne and Tessa in 1999.

Scott still urges young dancers to continue in singles as long as they can and feels that's even more important with the demanding technically based skill sets required under the code of points judging system, which was implemented in 2004.

In Waterloo, they learned essential fundamentals of body positioning, edge quality, speed, and blade control from Paul. "I was training Danny then, and one thing about the Moirs: they're real boys," Paul says. "They're kind of crazy and out there, but are very willing to participate in things that are not just simple training. I tried to keep Scott under control with his training so later in life he'd be good at it, and it worked. He's a training animal now. I was the technician and Suzanne was the creative force."

While Paul pushed them in the discipline of technique, Suzanne pushed them even harder on the artistic side of ice dancing.

"Suz had us trying crazy things: trying to twizzle as fast as possible and doing dips and fun moves and really creative things," recalls Tessa, who revelled in the process. "We were doing things that were probably too advanced for our skill level, but at the same time it was a real challenge. That made us better and it made it really fun. She'd show us something and ask, 'Can you do that?' And we'd think she was crazy because there was no way we were doing footwork and changes that fast. For so long, we couldn't do it but we'd just work away and get better. Doing those things that were advanced and different and creative, I really think that those early programs started us off right."

With Tessa's affinity for choreography and love of dance, she was immediately drawn to Suzanne and, despite their age difference, the feeling was mutual. At a party in Ilderton to celebrate the 1999 novice title won by Sheri and Danny Moir, Suzanne and Tessa spent most of the evening together on the dance floor creating an add-on dance, where one person does four steps, the other adds four more, and so on. "I thought, 'This is the start of a really good friendship,'" Suzanne says.

If Suzanne and Paul split their coaching team roughly along technical and creative lines, their dance team did the same thing. Scott, through practice and DNA, was firmly grounded in "pure skating," while Tessa's background in ballet and modern dance ignited her interest in the choreographic side.

"For sure," she says. "Choreography comes naturally to Scott too, but he's more technical," Tessa says. "I might say to him, 'So, I want to hover around you like a butterfly,' and he could figure out how to make it work. But he's also so musical, and he's not even conscious of it."

In fact, Scott has often been compared to four-time world champion Kurt Browning in that sense: a skater who at the beginning of his career was known mostly for his technical and athletic

"[SCOTT IS] MORE TECHNICAL.
I MIGHT SAY TO HIM, 'SO, I WANT TO HOVER AROUND
YOU LIKE A BUTTERFLY,' AND HE COULD FIGURE OUT
HOW TO MAKE IT WORK." — *Tessa*

Above: Posing on the ice during a photoshoot, 2000.

prowess, but who had a natural feel for music and artistry that began to exhibit itself as he became more mature. Over time, Scott became a larger contributor to the choreographic process and Tessa went through a similar growth process on the technical side, but in their early years in Waterloo they were guided by their natural tendencies. The most dominant of those tendencies was their competitiveness, both as a team and as individuals. That was an important asset because it kept both of them striving to become better, eliminating one of the major causes of dance and pairs teams splitting up: an inequality of ability. Almost no championship couple, outside of brother-sister teams,

They became the fastest, a process that had started a few years earlier. Paul and Suzanne had a "tween" couple on their hands who were fast, naturally talented, born performers, competitive with themselves and with each other, driven to win, and respectful of their coaches' abilities.

"They always understood, and took what you were saying and applied it," Suzanne says. "There was an acceptance of what you said, and they just did it. Normally kids have excuses; that it's too hard, their partner isn't ready, they don't have the confidence. But their friendship together, to really know that your partner is there for you, instills a confidence that most partnerships don't have.

"WE WERE ALWAYS THE SMALLEST AND WE ALWAYS MADE A POINT OF PROVING THAT WE WEREN'T THE SLOWEST." —*Scott*

start as young and last as long as Tessa and Scott have. Often, the best duos are assembled after it has become clear they will be of roughly equal calibre.

"There was a time when Scott was light years ahead of me," Tessa says. "And there was also a time when everyone was worried that I was going to outgrow Scott. In those early years I always felt like I was playing catch-up. Until our early teens, I would say."

"I felt exactly the same way," Scott says, with some amazement. "I felt like I was always a step behind you. And I had to step it up. I remember that feeling, but I never remember you having to catch up at all. We were very blessed in both of those areas: we pretty much grew together."

"Another part of it was that, until very recently, we were always the smallest team," Tessa adds. "The tiniest. Immature and young. Maybe that pushed us because we always felt we had something to prove."

"We were always the smallest," adds Scott, "and we always made a point of proving that we weren't the slowest."

They had problems like any other partnership, but they knew they were committed and they had a willingness to believe. That trust grows over the years, but I think you have to come built that way in the first place."

The fact that they were winning competitions helped reinforce the trust in each other and in their coaches. As soon as they were juvenile champions, they set their sights on the pre-novice title, even though the age gap between them and most of the other teams would be even wider than it had been in juvenile. In 2001, Tomorrow's Champions was held at the Kitchener Auditorium, an older, intimate arena known as "The Aud." Tessa and Scott weren't expected to win; traditionally ice dancers rarely triumphed in their first year at any level, even if they were the best on that particular evening. But Tessa and Scott defied the odds — and history — and won the pre-novice championship over a field of older opponents. In the process, they gave their first of what would eventually become hundreds of TV interviews. Immediately, they reset their sights

Opposite: On the ice during a competition.
Above: With medals at Skate Canada Junior National Competition, 2001.
Below: A television interview with local media.

Above: Tessa and Scott wearing "Canada" athletic clothing.
Opposite: On the ice during a competition, 2002.

to focus on the novice ranks they would move into for the 2001–2 season. They remained focused on the task at hand and never thought of how they were rocketing toward the upper echelons of Canadian skating, or of what was happening on the international scene they might be joining one day.

"We saw what we were chasing," Scott shrugs. "We didn't really see past that at all, which is probably a good thing. I don't think we ever compared ourselves to the world champions of the time. But every competition we were in, I'd go out there and say to myself, 'How can I compete against these guys?' And then we would compete and beat them."

They were about to enter novice skating, which in ice dancing meant a dramatic change in approach. For the first time they would be required — or, from their viewpoint, finally be allowed — to perform a regular free skate in competition. As well, ice dancing's hierarchy and "protocol judging" (keeping skaters in the spot they're expected to finish) tend to kick in at the novice level. Most couples were expected to spend at least two years in novice before they'd get to the

podium, and move up to another three years at junior before finally reaching senior skating. "And that's the good ones," Carol Moir says. That delayed process was expected to be even more pronounced for a couple who would be only twelve and fourteen when the 2002 novice championships in Newfoundland rolled around.

"We used that protocol thing in their training," Suzanne remembers. "For motivation and planning and to stretch them we would say: 'We'll go out and do everything we can and *dare* them not to put us first.' It's not that they expected to finish first, but we wanted to get people wondering why they didn't."

At the same time, Suzanne was working diligently at getting Tessa and Scott to fully understand each other and what they had together. She would hold regular meetings where each partner could clear the air, or grapple out loud with something that had been bothering them. Those meetings continued until they were well beyond their mid-teens, proving to be invaluable both then and later on in their careers.

"I'd try to make them understand that any relationship, marriage, business partnership, skating partnership, whatever, is a challenge," Suzanne explains. "When you get young people working toward a common goal that's very important. I tried to get them to appreciate each other as individuals, to know that they needed each other and that it didn't matter if one had excelled at something and the other didn't. They were in it together."

Tessa and Scott already had the natural tendency to treat each other with respect and affection, but as Tessa recalls, "We were young teenagers, a boy and a girl trying to work together as a team. So that's when we started figuring out what the other brings to the relationship and, well, not fighting, but we were banging up against each other."

"We were starting to be opinionated," Scott says. "I remember when I was a young boy and I'd see the older guys fighting with their partners. It took a couple of years to figure out that was not the way it should be. We never really fought on the ice, but Suzanne was a big part of getting through that stage and making us realize that we're both in it for the same reasons, that we need to work

together on the ice, and that it's important to get along. And that's something we carried with us all the way through."

"On the ice we're together," Tessa adds, "but off the ice we continued to grow in different directions, so Suz sat us down once or twice a week and we'd review things: She'd ask, 'Tell me how this made you feel when he said this,' or, 'Scott, how did you feel when she did this?' Suz can really take credit for helping us get our business relationship and our working relationship straight. We had to learn that distinction at a very young age, and she gave us the opportunity to talk about things and feel open. It's a part of our relationship people

don't see. It is like a marriage in the sense that it takes a lot of work, and that was a big part of who we became. And no one knows that. Everyone knows that we're best friends now but with all those transitions that you're going through individually and as you're trying to make it work on the ice, there were times we didn't get along. We're such different people in the way we handle things. It's taken almost until now to know exactly how we each deal with things and how to respond accordingly. I learned then that because Scott is so passionate and so intense — I mean, he's a goofy guy and fun-loving, but on the ice he's so intense and takes things so seriously — that sometimes if things

aren't working he just needs to blow off steam. Whether that means skating away or yelling or kicking the ice or whatever. Scott wears his feelings on his sleeve."

Tessa admits that at certain points in their pre- and early teen years they were both scared that the partnership might not succeed.

"We had a rough patch," she said. "Now we know that when you're together for so long, there are some ups and downs. But at the time you think, 'Can we work together? Is this going to happen?'"

"Tessa is able to put her emotions aside and think practically," Scott says. Tessa will say, "'Okay, it didn't go well but let's fix it so next time it will

go well.' Over the years I've tried to pick that up because it makes more sense. My natural reaction would be to just go nuts. Go wild, shut down, and get mad."

In Waterloo, they began to recognize that while what they shared — natural chemistry, steadfast friendship, competitive drive, devotion to improving every day — was their greatest strength, how they differed also helped produce a more complete partnership. Essentially, Tessa says, he brings the passion and energy, and she has a calming effect. And such contrasts are usually at the root of all great art.

Even though Tessa and Scott were just twelve and fourteen, Suzanne knew that she had to design a mature free skating program for them as they prepared for their first novice season.

"We were competing with people who are portraying adults," Tessa explains.

Suzanne chose the Cancan, loaded it with fast footwork, and combined two difficult pieces of music, the first of which was a tango. "People doubted the choice of the tango," she recalls. "It's a mature dance, and they were really young and two feet high."

Tessa loved it. Always advanced choreographically, she embraced the "adultness" of the program. They were young, and looked it, and were still worried about her growing too tall, but they had taken a big step forward. They weren't projecting "cute" any more, they were projecting intimacy.

"The tango was the first program in which we had our foreheads together, and we were getting closer to moves that older skaters were doing," she says. "And it had the fastest footwork we'd ever tried to do, or even seen. Although we didn't know it at the time, I think that made a difference in the larger scheme of things because the tango has such a quick tempo, but you also have to be intimate. We really started to get the flavour of it."

Left: A break during practice.
Above: (left to right) Danny, Tessa, Jordan, and Scott.
Right: Scott at the top of the podium.

Opposite: Travelling in Vienna.
Above: With Suzanne at novice
invitational in Vienna, Austria, 2000.
Below: On the ice, during
competition in Vienna.

And the tango called for a lot of on-ice act-ing beyond their years. They were portraying fully developed characters. Many fourteen-year-old boys would not have been able to find the abandon to allow themselves to become the character Scott had to play.

"Suzanne was great with me," Scott recalls. "She would tell me what she thought the part should be and she would give me an avenue, so that I could express what she wanted, but in my own way. I had a lot of help. Trying to keep up with Tessa's expressiveness was tough."

But he managed it. They travelled to Newfoundland for Tomorrow's Champions with the Canadian skating community anticipating that they would make an impression — staking out future ground, but certainly not reaching the podium. Once again, they outstripped expecta-tions and finished a close third. "They fell," Paul MacIntosh says, "or they could have finished first."

Scott was angry about not winning the title and wanted to return to novice the next season to capture gold. But Paul and Suzanne had already decided they should fast-track the team to junior. "Don't hold these kids back," Suzanne advised. Alma Moir, though, was against the jump, worrying that they were "so little" for junior skating. But as she had said before, they were skating big.

Shortly after Tomorrow's Champions, the Western Ontario Section sent Tessa and Scott to a novice invitational in Vienna, their first overseas event. It wasn't an official International Skating Union (ISU) event, but many European dance offi-cials were in attendance. Scott calls it the worst competition of their lives because they hadn't really trained for it: "We skated the first forty sec-onds well and then ten seconds into the Cancan, it fell apart. We were winning after compulsories in the first European competition of our lives. We had a slip-up in the free dance and then just chased each other around the ice for the next minute. It was *embarrassing.* First in compulsories, fourth overall."

The winners were talented Americans Meryl Davis, two years older than Tessa, and Charlie White, six weeks younger than Scott. They didn't foresee it then, but the two couples would go head-to-head

"'THERE'S NO REASON — AS LONG AS TESSA DOESN'T GROW TOO MUCH — THAT THESE TWO CAN'T BE AT THE OLYMPICS IN 2010.'"—*Suzanne Killing*

several more times over the next eight years, on the biggest skating stages the world has to offer.

While the skaters were disappointed in their performance in Vienna, their coaches were not. They felt the program created a buzz and "captured so many eyes."

The 2001–2 season — an Olympic year that produced the pairs judging scandal in Salt Lake City that was linked to vote-buying in the ice dance event — was drawing to a close. Tessa and Scott had now arrived at a crossroads, and had a difficult decision to make. They were about to enter junior competition, in which the best skaters were training full time, five days a week, several hours a day. Tessa and Scott couldn't afford that kind of time, and couldn't spend so many hours commuting. She was about to enter her final year of elementary

school, and he'd just had the "best year" of his school life as a freshman at Medway High School in nearby Arva, but they knew they couldn't properly pursue their goals if they kept on as they were. So, at the annual Virtue-Moir meeting, the families agreed: Tessa and Scott had to move to Waterloo.

Something else was brought up for the first time that spring, something that might have been brewing in the minds of Tessa and Scott but hadn't been mentioned aloud.

"Jim Virtue wanted to see the ultimate plan," Suzanne says, recalling that everyone knew Vancouver was bidding to host the 2010 Winter Games, but that the site had not yet been chosen.

"And I said to him, 'There's no reason — as long as Tessa doesn't grow too much — that these two can't be at the Olympics in 2010.'"

"It was like we were on this little adventure. You're with a team, you get the Canada jackets, and you're travelling: you're thirteen years old and you're going to see Slovakia, Croatia, and Holland." — *Tessa*

Chapter Three

THE CLASS OF THE ICE

THE YOUNG COUPLE FACED DIFFICULT CHALLENGES, BUT THEY WERE SUSTAINED BY THEIR LOVE FOR SKATING AND THE KNOWLEDGE THAT THEY COULD BE CHAMPIONS.

TESSA LIKES THE AGE-OLD DESCRIPTION OF a duck: calm on the surface, but paddling like the dickens underneath. It speaks to the art of making tortuous ice dancing manoeuvres look easy and pleasurable, and it also describes how, on the way to medals and championships, skaters must make great sacrifices and overcome serious obstacles that the public knows nothing about.

Moving away from home is never easy, at any age, but when you're entering the teen years, the most social part of your life, it's particularly difficult to leave family and friends to move to another city. But Tessa and Scott had to face that painful separation in September 2002 when they left London and Ilderton to enroll at Bluevale Collegiate Institute in Waterloo, Ontario.

They were both billeting in excellent family situations: Scott with Bev and Grace Strachan, and Tessa joining fellow ice dancer Bronwyn Williams at the home of Kitchener-Waterloo skating club coach Becky Babb and her husband Scott Strachan. That eased the worry for the Moir and Virtue families, and so did the knowledge that, as Alma Moir describes it, "Tessa and Scott could look out for each other."

Still, there were a lot of adjustments for thirteen- and fifteen-year-olds.

Left: Tessa and Scott posing for a photo before travelling to a competition. *Opposite:* Tessa and Scott attending a banquet dinner held during a competition in Andorra, 2005.

"It was a big time of our lives and we were both scared," Scott concedes. "We were together a lot during that time. Not only were we skating partners, but we were really each other's family because we were more or less alone in Kitchener-Waterloo."

Tessa should have still been in elementary school, but she was a good student and received permission from London's Stoneybrook Public School to skip grade eight and enter high school a year early. (She did return to London at the end of the year to watch from the audience as the kids she'd known since kindergarten graduated from

Above: With coach Paul MacIntosh.
Opposite: Tessa and Scott enjoy some free time outdoors.

grade eight. It was difficult for her, her mother recalls, but education and friends are important to Tessa and she wanted to be there for their big day.)

"We were already comfortable in the rink setting in Waterloo because we had been commuting," Tessa recalls. "School was the biggest thing. There were so many skaters who would go from the rink right to the high school. It sounds funny now, but that was basically why I skipped grade eight, so I could get rides with them, and so I could have first-period spare and skate in the morning.

"I remember the first day of grade nine very well: I was missing two teeth, I was walking up these big steps to what seemed like a huge school, I didn't know anyone, didn't know where I was going, didn't know what classes I was taking and I

was feeling like I was missing out because I didn't get the grade eight experience. I remember sitting by myself at lunch before I made any friends. And Scott and I were going home on weekends, so we weren't around to socialize then. I think girls are different that way. If you miss one minute of the weekend time then you're out of the loop and I felt out of the loop going in. Grade nine was tough, but grade ten was my favourite year. By then it was home to me and I was comfortable and made so many friends. And I actually went back to that prom when they all graduated, even though I only went there for grade nine and ten."

Scott had spent grade nine at Medway High School in Arva, Ontario, about eight kilometres from Bethel Church, where he and Tessa had passed four years waiting for each other to go to pre-dawn practices.

"Ninth grade was the best year I can remember. At the end of that year I was sad, because I knew I wanted to get better at skating and I wanted to push to the next level of junior, but that meant I would have to leave. That was tough, but it was worth it. When you're a kid, high school's the thing and if you're not there you think you're missing out on so much. At Bluevale I had one friend who was also a skater (Andrew Poje), so I hung out with him. I met almost no one in tenth grade because I didn't want to make new friends, because I already had my friends at home. They were all city kids in Waterloo, and I missed my country buddies."

Tessa and Scott never had the same lunch periods, so he was unable to help her with that first-year lunchtime loneliness, but otherwise they spent more time than ever together, further solidifying an already sturdy friendship. Their lockers were right next to each other. Tessa would encourage Scott with his schoolwork, "and when I'd get down she'd help me. And sometimes the other way around."

A month before school started, Tessa and Scott took care of some unfinished business by winning the Lake Placid International novice dance competition. The previous summer, they had competed in their first international at Lake Placid,

"IT WAS A BIG TIME OF
OUR LIVES AND WE WERE
BOTH SCARED. WE WERE
TOGETHER A LOT DURING
THAT TIME. NOT ONLY
WERE WE SKATING PARTNERS,
BUT WE WERE REALLY
EACH OTHER'S FAMILY
BECAUSE WE WERE MORE
OR LESS ALONE IN
KITCHENER-WATERLOO." —*Scott*

Above: Performing compulsory dance program.
Opposite: During competition at the Lake Placid International dance competition, 2002.

the famous Adirondack site of two Winter Olympics. They'd finished third, but the two memories that linger for them are the excitement of hearing "Canada" after their names for the first time when they were introduced to skate and getting the little Canadian flag stickers attached to their skate boots.

They had been launched into the junior ranks because Paul and Suzanne wanted to keep challenging them and junior offered what novice didn't: the Original Dance (OD) program. It's the middle of the three ice dance segments, and corresponds to the short program in singles and pairs. The technical elements are dictated by the rules, and each year the ISU ice dance technical committee selects a rhythm that all couples must use, but the program design is left to the individual couples.

Suzanne designed a waltz OD, skated to Bach's "Les Poissons" from the Disney movie *The Little Mermaid* for their first year in junior. Paul still considers it among her best pieces of work. Tessa loved it, "because of the dress mostly," she laughs. "I like fashion, for sure, but when it comes down to it I like elegant things, classical things. And that carries over onto the ice. Scott likes to wear something pretty simple when he's skating."

"I'm just a basic guy, I guess," Scott quips. "She always looks wonderful so there's no need for me to."

That relatively simple elegance quickly became their trademark costume style — Suzanne made some of Tessa's costumes in those years — but there's far more to it than just personal preference. Since the early 1990s ice dancing, particularly in the international arena, had begun to resemble a high-end Halloween party, with costuming often overshadowing the athletic components of the performance.

"We had this understanding with Suzanne and with Paul that we wanted to let our skating speak for itself on the ice," Tessa confirms. "It's who we are as people as well."

The young Canadians could let their skating speak for itself because it had a strong and pure voice. It focused on the lower body;

the superb control of their blade edges; precise, quick transitions; knees as soft as cotton batten; and ever-increasing speed.

Paul knew that "Tessa and Scott would suffer for a year," with the jump to junior skating, and he was right. Smaller and younger than the rest of the competitors in the field, they finished seventh at Nationals in Saskatoon.

"The step up to junior was huge," Scott recalls. "This was the big Nationals."

Although they finished seventh, it was a very positive experience. Tessa fondly recalls sitting in the area where skaters wait for their marks to appear on the scoreboard (commonly known as the "kiss and cry") at a senior nationals for the first time, excitedly repeating, "That was so much fun, that was so much fun," after the Original Dance. "We loved to skate in front of people," she says, which would have come as no surprise to Alma Moir, who recalls that even when they were very young "the more crowded the arena was and the noisier it was, the more they both liked it. I once told Scott if skating didn't work out maybe he could be an actor."

Tessa remembers sitting by the boards when the senior dancers were doing their Golden Waltzes. "It was so fast. There was wind every time they skated by. That was the first time we'd watched a senior event live. They were so big, so fast."

And so accessible.

"We were riding the elevator with Marie-France and Patrice, and I nudged Tess and said, 'Hey, check it out.'"

"And Shae-Lynn and Victor," Tessa adds.

Canadian ice dancers Marie-France Dubreuil and Patrice Lauzon won five national titles and were silver medallists at the 2006 and 2007 world championships before retiring and getting married. Shae-Lynn Bourne and Victor Kraatz would go from their tenth national title in Saskatoon to winning the world championships in Washington less than two months later. Their victory over reigning champions Irina Lobacheva and Ilia Averbukh was a major turning point in ice dancing history. It was the first time since ice dancing had become an official world

Left: In Croatia, 2003.

championship discipline in 1952 that a couple from anywhere other than Europe had taken gold. And since 1970, Russian couples had dominated the discipline. Although five other non-Russians did win titles in the next thirty-three years, only Jayne Torvill and Christopher Dean, widely considered to be the greatest ice dancers of all time, made a significant dent in Russian domination of the event. Bourne and Kraatz's silver medal in 2002 was the highest finish by any team from North America in thirty-two years, although many skating insiders felt that Canada's Tracy Wilson and Rob McCall deserved at least one world championship (1988), and that

ately concentrating only on the junior teams directly in front of them.

One of those teams was Siobhan Karam and Joshua McGrath, who were junior bronze medallists in 2003 and would enter the following season as the favourites. They trained in Michigan under Russian expatriates Igor Shpilband, a former world junior ice dance champion, and Marina Zoueva, who had spent many years living and coaching in Ottawa. With Tessa and Scott planning a Russian medley free dance for the 2003–4 season, Paul asked Marina if she would spend some time with his couple to work on the authenticity of their

> "WE HAD THIS UNDERSTANDING WITH SUZANNE AND WITH PAUL THAT WE WANTED TO LET OUR SKATING SPEAK FOR ITSELF ON THE ICE. IT'S WHO WE ARE AS PEOPLE AS WELL." — *Tessa*

Bourne and Kraatz could have had one or two before they created history in Washington. But ice dancing, with far fewer falls than the other disciplines, was prey to more subjective judging, which in turn could often lead to "protocol judging" and, at worst, deal-making.

But none of that mattered to Tessa and Scott; it wasn't even on their radar. As they grew into their ice dancing careers, Canada had three world-class teams — Shae-Lynn Bourne and Victor Kraatz; Marie-France Dubreuil and Patrice Lauzon; and Megan Wing and Aaron Lowe — and an American couple, Ben Agosto skating with transplanted Canadian Tanith Belbin, were making a meteoric rise up the junior ranks. "Until after our own Olympics we never really put it together that none of them had ever won an Olympics," Scott said. Furthermore, Tessa and Scott were deliber-

dance. "I took them to Marina and she kind of played with them for a day, and she was brilliant with them," Paul recalls. "I knew they'd be direct competition to Siobhan and Josh the next junior Nationals, even if Marina and Igor didn't."

Officials at Skate Canada must have sensed something too. After finishing only seventh in their junior debut, Tessa and Scott were hoping to receive a junior Grand Prix assignment for the 2003 fall season. But they were scheduled for two Grand Prix events: Skate Slovakia in Bratislava in mid-September, and the Croatia Cup in Zagreb a month later. There was also the possibility of junior Worlds in The Hague in early March. Before any of those events, though, they were assigned to the North American Challenge Cup in the late summer in Thornhill, Ontario, a suburb bordering Toronto's northern limits. They won handily, as

Opposite: Hugging on the ice at Nationals, 2004. *Above:* With Paul during the 2003–2004 season.

Above and left:
A meal at the airport before leaving for competition.

they were impressed with the way their children skated in their first major international, they also "saw how young they were compared to everyone else," Alma explains. For instance, both the gold and silver medallist teams were made up of men and women who would be nineteen before the calendar year was out. The parents were concerned about their barely teenaged kids, "so Kate and I made a pact that there'd always be one parent who would go to the events."

Moreover, Bratislava just happened to be where the ISU dance committee was staging a weekend seminar to help judges prepare for the radical new "International Judging System," which had been fast-tracked after the judging scandal at the 2002 Olympic Games.

Canadian dancers took four of the top five spots in the cross-border junior competition.

"It was like we were on this little adventure," Tessa said. "You're with a team, you get the Canada jackets, and you're travelling: you're thirteen years old and you're going to see Slovakia, Croatia, and Holland."

Scott points out that once skaters reach senior they don't get to visit many of the countries they'd see on the Junior Grand Prix circuit, because they're not part of skating's Big Six — Russia, China, Japan, Canada, the United States, and France — which play host to the senior Grand Prix events.

At the first Junior Grand Prix event of their careers in Slovakia, Tessa and Scott finished sixth. But the ultimate importance of Skate Slovakia to Tessa and Scott's career could not be measured by placement. For one thing, both Alma Moir and Kate Virtue had travelled to Bratislava, and while

For more than a century, skating had used the heavily subjective 6.0 marking system through which judges were able to defend questionable rankings to referees with little more than "I liked them better." ISU president Ottavio Cinquanta demanded a more objective system, and put pressure on his staff to accelerate the process after the embarrassment of the judging scandal in Salt Lake City. The new and fundamentally different system, most of it designed and perfected in Canada, was to come into use for the 2004 Worlds and Grand Prix events. Canada would introduce it for the 2005 Nationals. It is a complex, computer-based concept, but the founding principle is that almost every element or movement of a program is marked against an established standard, not against other skaters. There are certain "levels" of skills, identified by "callers" who sit near the judging panel. Skaters start their program at zero and have points added for what they've done rather than starting at 6.0

Above: With Paul MacIntosh in Bratislava, Slovakia, 2003. *Bottom right:* Alma Moir and Kate Virtue in Slovakia.
Bottom left: Team Canada, *(back row, left to right):* Carol Hopper, John Mattatall, Christopher Maybee, Cedric Demers, Scott; *(front row):* Dr. Susan Blatz, Megan Duhamel, Ashton Tessier, Tessa, and Terra Findlay.

and having points subtracted on some undefined basis. A computer randomly selects which judges' scores will count in the official tally. And individual judges are never identified by their marks, which might increase public suspicion, but protects the judges from the deal-making, and anger, of their own skating federations. (There have been many instances of a federation asking its own judges to go against their consciences and give a higher or lower mark to particular skaters, just to accommodate a deal.)

The new system was made to be far more objective, it was made to reward performance rather than reputation, and it was made to encourage faster, more all-round skating skills.

In short, it was tailor-made for Tessa Virtue and Scott Moir, who were fast, energetic, and well-grounded in every aspect of ice dancing, and clearly upwardly mobile.

Their Original Dance during the 2003 season was a combination of the classic 1950s rock tunes "Tears on My Pillow" and "Tutti Frutti" and contained the usual speed and difficult footwork.

"Two delegates from the ISU committee, from Italy and Ukraine, stormed through people to find me," Paul MacIntosh recalls. "Just to say that Tessa and Scott's OD was exactly the way the committee had envisioned things for the new system."

Whatever the scoring system, it can never hurt skaters to have judges believing that they're the ones who are capable of satisfying it.

THE NEXT MONTH, TESSA AND SCOTT WERE fourth at the Croatia Cup. They returned to Kitchener for more intense training, then headed to Edmonton in January for the Nationals. They were no longer in awe of the competition and won the title. Looking back, Tessa and Scott recognize that was a pivotal moment in their careers. Winning the Nationals sent them to international events as champions of a major skating nation, and gave

them enormous confidence, and established them as a team on a meteoric rise. They were named to the team for junior Worlds at The Hague in early March, but first they travelled to Halifax to spend a few days with Suzanne, who had left Waterloo to begin studies in psychology at Dalhousie University. She fine-tuned their programs and it was off to their first Junior Worlds, where they finished a respectable eleventh. Scott felt they skated reasonably well and was most encouraged by their solid free dance, which would provide them a tailwind heading into the next season, when they would begin yet another climb: this time up the senior ranks.

Above: Spending time with Suzanne in Halifax, 2004.

"That was probably my favourite competition," Tessa recalls. "My entire family was there, and we went to Amsterdam afterward. It seemed like more than a competition."

For Paul it was finally time to take a breather and reflect upon how far his young team had come in less than a year: "We had been working at this a long time, but it was a real whirlwind of seven months when they took skating by storm. They were eleventh at Junior Worlds, but you knew they were better than eleventh and they would certainly surpass the other competitors."

Those were prophetic words, but by the time they came true Tessa and Scott would no longer be skating in Waterloo or with Paul as their coach.

That spring, after six years of working in Waterloo and two years of living there full-time, Tessa and Scott decided they needed to change training venues. Suzanne had already moved to Halifax, removing a piece of the coaching equation that had worked so well. And even Paul concedes that while he was doing well with other teams without Suzanne, "I probably couldn't have done it with those two."

"At that time we were basically the top team in Waterloo," Tessa explains. "There weren't the big star teams ahead of us that were motivating us. We grew up with that, and it makes a big difference in the training atmosphere. We needed to go somewhere where there were teams that were better than us."

1990. Marina had worked as a choreographer with the incomparable pairs skaters Ekaterina Gordeeva and Sergei Grinkov, the legendary husband and wife duo who won two Olympic championships. She was on the ice in Moscow the day they first skated together in 1981, and was the only other person on the Lake Placid practice ice with "G & G" in November 1995 when Sergei collapsed and died.

"Even the first time Tessa and Scott came to Michigan just to try us as coaches, I felt their spirit, the same spirit, the same image as Katia and Sergei," Zoueva once told the *Hamilton Spectator* "Man and woman on ice. The chemistry. Man and woman in sync. It has never happened in ice dance before like this. Our sport with the new judging system is 50 percent sport, 50 percent art, and this pair represents that harmony."

"THERE WEREN'T THE BIG STAR TEAMS AHEAD OF US THAT WERE MOTIVATING US. WE GREW UP WITH THAT, AND IT MAKES A BIG DIFFERENCE IN THE TRAINING ATMOSPHERE. WE NEEDED TO GO SOMEWHERE WHERE THERE WERE TEAMS THAT WERE BETTER THAN US." *— Tessa*

They were prepared to test drive a number of different coaching situations and decided to start with Canton, Michigan, because they had already worked with Marina Zoueva and because it was only two and a half hours from their western Ontario homes. They went to Michigan for a couple of days, felt they could work with Marina and her coaching partner Igor Shpilband, and agreed to return for another two-week stretch after school was over for the summer. Tessa sensed that Marina and Igor were also testing them out a bit too, gauging them as potential students.

"We liked it, so we didn't have to try anywhere else," Scott says. "They were good about it. We had just beaten their team, Siobhan and Josh, but Marina and Igor said, 'We'd love to have you.'"

Igor had won the 1983 world junior ice dance championship with Tatiana Gladkova, skating for the old Soviet Union, but he defected to the U.S. in

Many top North American couples were already training with Marina and Igor, including Canadian silver medallists Megan Wing and Aaron Lowe and American champions Tanith Belbin and Ben Agosto, who would eventually win an Olympic silver medal and four medals at Worlds.

Moving to Waterloo at the ages of thirteen and fifteen, then travelling to Europe to compete, made it slightly easier for Tessa and Scott to move again at fifteen and seventeen, but it was still a major adjustment. If they were looking for a big change, they certainly found it. The skating style Marina and Igor taught was different than they were used to and took some adjustments on Tessa and Scott's part. And Tessa, who is always concerned for the feelings of others, would have felt a certain disloyalty to Suzanne and Paul if she had quickly embraced the new training environment.

"I just needed to get to know people and get comfortable. It took a couple of months."

"I JUST NEEDED TO GET TO KNOW PEOPLE AND GET COMFORTABLE. IT TOOK A COUPLE OF MONTHS." —*Tessa*

After so long with Paul and Suzanne, Tessa and Scott had become accustomed to a warm personal relationship with their coaches. The Michigan school was more formal, with more of a barrier between coach and student. Although their relationship with Marina and Igor has since evolved to the point that it's almost a four-person coaching team, the young Canadians, already somewhat intimidated by the setting, were taken aback by the directness, and occasional yelling, of their new coaches.

"They were a lot more aggressive," Scott says. "They don't do subtle. They don't mince words; they don't beat around the bush."

"It took a lot of getting used to," Tessa continues, "especially for me. I want to please. I want them to be happy and I want to do the right thing. And when you don't get that feedback — I think that's what I struggled with at the beginning. It was more rigid, the roles are clear. That's actually great and we really appreciate it now."

Scott moved in with one of the coaches, Brandon Forsyth, and Tessa roomed with pairs skater Tiffany Stiegler, who was five years older. Until Kate Virtue joined her daughter in Canton eight months later, Scott, who had a car, would drive Tessa to the rink, grocery store, and home to western Ontario for the weekends. The three hours they'd spend in the car together, talking about everything but skating, further deepened an already deep relationship.

As they slowly grew more comfortable in their new surroundings, Tessa and Scott were sustained by their love for skating and the knowledge that this was the training ground where they could become national, and perhaps world and Olympic champions. They were stimulated by the contagious energy that bristled through the busy arena from six in the morning until six at night.

They would be competing as seniors at the 2005 Canadian championships (in, of all places, London, Ontario), but they would spend that Grand Prix season, and the one after it, on the junior circuit. That meant balancing training to embrace both competition levels. The junior free skate, for instance, is a three-minute event, while

Above: Tessa and Scott enjoying free time. *Below:* Sightseeing in Courcheval, France, 2004. *Opposite:* Tessa during a training session, 2004.

Above: Celebrating their silver medal win at the Junior Grand Prix competition in Courcheval.

seniors free skate for four minutes. The new scoring system, which would eventually be called the Code of Points, was introduced to Grand Prix skating that fall and Nationals in January.

"We liked it right away," Scott says of the new scoring system. "We liked the feedback, how people were getting rewarded for what they were doing. And how clear the levels were. They still had some kinks to work out, but I liked how you could move so much. If you were fourth in compulsories, you could still move up and be first overall. And it was easy for us to see where we could improve. That's one of the best things about the new system. You know exactly where you need to change things and where you can get more points.

"Ever since that season we looked at the marks sheet and said, 'Okay, we're only eleventh right here. Why? Let's fix that and get 'em higher.'"

So Tessa and Scott embraced the Code of Points from its inception, and so did their coaches,

who always stayed on top of the requirements and the annual changes the ISU would make to them. So from the start of the new system, the entire team was ahead of the game rather than trying to catch up to it.

Igor's main focus in the couple's first year with him was to continue to increase their speed and power. "When they came to us, they were still a junior team and they weren't the biggest team or the fastest team and I told them 'you need to become the fastest,' because I thought that was what they needed most," recalls Igor. "I worked with them on basic skating technique. When you have good control and feel secure on your feet, you feel you can go faster.

"They impressed me right away with their ability to relate to each other, their ability to dance, and the difficult things they could do on the ice. And they were very fluid. One of the things they were lacking was the power."

Above: Tessa and Scott after their Grand Prix victory in China, 2004.

Working hard on their speed and their power Tessa and Scott were soon on their way to becoming the fastest dance team in the world.

In those first few months Igor was learning as much about his new students as they were about him. "First of all, they're very bright kids," he says. "They know exactly what they want and what they need. They're very aware at the rink. They know what everyone is doing around them, they're so tuned in with what goes on with every single person on the ice. That sharpness and awareness really helps them. They're very comfortable on the ice, they're secure on the ice and secure with each other.

"When they first arrived I asked what they should skate their free dance to and they wanted a tango. When they played the piece ("Adios Nonino") for me, I felt it was one you have to be very mature for. There are a lot of very sophisticated tango couples who wouldn't use it, it's so difficult. But they said, 'we want to do it.' So that was the first free dance I choreographed for them. I thought they were too young to show sophisticated emotion. You don't often find that understanding of music and dance from kids that age."

But with increasing speed and power, they mastered the difficult tango and headed out on the junior Grand Prix circuit.

Their first event was in Courcheval, France, in late August 2004. Tessa and Scott finished second to eventual world junior champions Morgan Matthews and Maxim Zavozin, but beat them in the free dance, a major indicator of their rising status and skill level because the free dance is worth as much in the scoring system as the compulsory and original dance combined.

Paul MacIntosh was also at Courcheval with Alice Graham and Andrew Poje. In practices, Tessa and Scott found it disconcerting to skate past his spot at the boards, where in the past they would have stopped for coaching directions.

"IT WAS THE LOUDEST I'D EVER HEARD AT A COMPETITION. AND
THIS WAS THE FIRST TIME THERE WERE SIGNS FOR US." —*Tessa*

While there had been some initial bitterness over their departure from Waterloo, Tessa and Scott were renewing their friendship with Paul. When they headed for their next Grand Prix in northern China — the first real competition of their career that he wouldn't be present for — Paul e-mailed his former students with a reminder of something he used to say to them years earlier: "Be the class of the ice." They won their China event, their first Grand Prix victory, and since then Paul has sent them a similar message before every competition. It is part motivation and part good luck charm, joining Scott's short list of superstitions — new socks for every event — and Tessa's long one: putting the left skate on first; setting her water bottle in the same place on the boards, with her skate guards at the same angle every time; taking the same route through a competition arena every day; keeping a safety pin, always head-up, stuck somewhere in her skating costume.

The first two junior Grand Prix medals of their career qualified them for December's Junior Grand Prix Final in Helsinki, Finland, where they finished second to Matthews and Zavozin, but once again beat them in the free dance. Then, after competing on three different continents that fall, they returned to their own backyard, their *two* backyards actually, with their first Canadian senior Nationals at London's John Labatt Centre, and the junior world championships at the Kitchener Auditorium. The next time they'd compete at the John Labatt Centre and The Aud in the same skating year would be the 2010 Olympic season. The Labatt Centre "was jammed to the rafters" for their January homecoming, Tessa recalls, "and it was the loudest I'd ever heard at a competition. And this was the first time there were signs for us. I'd be skating around going, 'Oh! That says our names on it.'"

Tessa had hoped they would break into senior with "a top ten finish," but, responding to an

Above: With Joe and Alma Moir. *Opposite:* Canadian senior Nationals competition, 2004.

adoring crowd, they finished fourth, three spots higher than they had managed in their national junior debut. Again, Tessa and Scott saved their best for last, finishing third in the free dance ahead of the ultimate bronze medallists.

The next month, feeling they had something to prove in Kitchener because of the recent switch in training locations, they finished a strong second at the world junior championships. Scott felt the judging panel "really hammered us" for a trip in the free dance. Nevertheless, a season that had opened amid anxiety and fear was closing with a silver medal and optimism, and Tessa and Scott assumed that they would move from the junior Grand Prix to the senior circuit. But in a reversal of their leap from novice to junior three years earlier, the skaters wanted to move up and the coaches wanted to hold them back. Marina and Igor prevailed and Tessa and Scott spent the 2005–6 international season as junior skaters again.

TESSA AND SCOTT HAD SETTLED INTO LIFE in Canton, grown accustomed to and embraced the coaching styles of Marina and Igor, and their spins and lifts coach, Johnny Johns, and their skating was thriving. They were on the ice for five hours a day, and Scott was coaching some of the younger students. Tessa, after encountering difficulties enrolling in a U.S. school because of visa issues and taking two online courses the first few months in Michigan, had enrolled at Holy Names High School in Windsor the previous January and was enjoying being back in class again. The only issue was that Holy Names students had to wear school uniforms. "So it was all about accessorizing," she laughs. Scott says he "still had some growing up to do, though. In the off-season, I was still breaking down over the Junior Worlds; I thought I'd let the team down when we really needed to skate the lights out. Marina said, 'What's wrong with you? It's

"WE HAD TO LEARN HOW
TO COMPETE, BEING THE FAVOURITES.
WE'D ALWAYS BEEN THE CHALLENGERS.
IT'S A TOTALLY DIFFERENT FEELING
BEING ON THE ICE WITH EVERYONE
COMING AFTER YOU." —*Tessa*

Right: On the ice at Skate Canada, 2006.
Below: At their hotel in Andorra, 2005.

over, you have to start thinking about the future. It's time to grow up and be a man.' In her heavy accent."

Tessa is quick to defend her partner: "In our minds we had decided, 'Okay, we'll win junior Worlds this year and then we'll go to senior Worlds. But we didn't win Junior Worlds and then Marina and Igor wanted us to stay in junior, so we kind of felt we had let ourselves down. We expected more of ourselves and it was the first time we had to deal with that kind of setback."

The young couple were used to exceeding expectations, including their own, and for part of the summer of 2005, "We thought our life was over, but it turned out it worked in our favour," Scott says. They eventually moved beyond their disappointment, and used it to fuel their motivation for another busy season. And, as the year progressed, they discovered their coaches were right in holding them back for the first time in their career.

"We had to learn how to compete, being the favourites," Tessa explains. "We'd always been the challengers. It's a totally different feeling being on the ice with everyone coming after you."

"And you have everything to lose," Scott continues. "It took a lot of getting used to. I was a lot more nervous that year but we did pretty well with it."

In fact, they went undefeated through the fall season, winning junior Grand Prix events in Montreal and Andorra within a three-week period in September and the Junior Grand Prix Final in the Czech Republic in November. And this was despite not being overly enthusiastic about the music for the free dance program. Tessa and Scott had learned from past experience that because they both put everything they have into their programs every day, they both have to like the music. But in the spring of 2005, the two coaches and the two skaters hadn't been able to come to a consensus about their music. Finally Igor said, "Time's up," and chose the music for them. Tessa and Scott never totally got the feel of the music, but it didn't prevent them from sweeping their fall events and coming into their second senior Nationals riding a tailwind.

They finished third at Nationals, but were second in both the OD and the free dance. "We thought, 'We're probably going to the Olympics because we were second in the two most important parts.' I guess that's what we went into Nationals thinking," Tessa recalls. But Skate Canada officials followed established protocol and named Dubreuil and Lauzon and silver medallists Wing and Lowe to the Olympics in Torino and the Worlds in Calgary.

"It was devastating to a sixteen-year-old," Tessa says. "Vancouver was four years away and we thought we needed to know what an Olympics is like. It was a huge disappointment and made me re-evaluate. I wasn't sure I was ready to put in another four years to get to an Olympics. But looking back it was the best thing that could have happened to us."

Just like Igor insisting that they stay at the junior level for an extra year of internationals, being passed over for the 2006 Olympic team eventually made Tessa and Scott even more determined. And Tessa now feels that had they gone to Worlds or Olympics, they would have had to move up slowly rather than using the experience and maturity of another year to make a more heralded and impressive world senior debut.

"It's funny, though, because people would ask me during the Vancouver Olympics if I was enjoying them more than the last ones," Scott laughs. "Well, yeah, I wasn't watching them in my living room!"

They still had junior Worlds in March to look forward to. And they dominated the competition that week in Lublijana, taking first in all three segments and amassing 172.57 points under the new judging system to become the first Canadian ice dancers ever to win the world junior title. In fact, Canada hadn't won a junior world championship in *any* discipline since 1978. Many observers felt bronze medallists Meryl Davis and Charlie White should have been second.

Meryl and Charlie, Michigan natives who had been together only a year less than Tessa and Scott, had moved from the Detroit Figure Skating Club earlier that year to work with Marina and Igor. Although they compete head-to-head and dominate their generation of ice dancers, the four skaters are friends, with Scott and Charlie particularly close.

Scott and Charlie both played competitive hockey well into their teens, and discovered by accident one day that they had played against each other in a tournament, with a bench-clearing brawl highlighting the game.

Before departing for Lublijana, Tessa and Scott had spent an eerie few weeks in Canton, as their coaches and three of the dance teams they trained closely with had all departed for the Olympics. But even that turned into a positive as Skate Canada's Marijane Stong, who had known Tessa and Scott since their very earliest competitions, came to Canton to fill the coaching void. She provided a different energy and a different set of eyes, but most importantly she introduced them to "key words."

"It's just an easy way for Tessa and I to communicate before we perform, without really talking," Scott explains.

"Something like 'knees' might really mean 'bend your knees,' or 'time' means 'we don't have anything to rush for,'" Tessa continues. "After the warmup, we talk through our whole program together and say, 'When we get to this point, we're going to think about this,' and we use our key words there. Then when we get on the ice and say those words, it clicks."

They use about fifteen of those key words, and it should come as no surprise that one is a particular favourite, for both of them: "Together."

Opposite top: With Meryl Davis and Charlie White in Andorra, 2005.
Opposite below: At Junior Worlds in Venice, 2005.
Opposite bottom and right: On the ice during competition in Andorra.

"WE WANTED IT SO BADLY.
MARINA AND IGOR
WANTED IT SO BADLY.
WE KNEW THE NEXT STEP
WAS WINNING." —*Tessa*

Chapter Four

ROAD TO GOLD

TESSA AND SCOTT WOULD OFTEN USE THE KEY WORDS "BEST IN THE WORLD" DURING PRACTICE. THAT MOTIVATED THEM TO TRAIN MORE INTENSELY THAN EVER BEFORE.

WHEN TESSA AND SCOTT WERE finally able to leave junior skating for good, as world champions, they also left behind the only season in which they had been the chased rather than the chasers.

In fall 2006, recovered from the disappointment of not being selected for the Torino Olympics and armed with two new programs, they were back to climbing their way up the ladder. Tessa was seventeen and Scott had just turned nineteen when they entered senior ranks full-time with their first Grand Prix appearance in Victoria, B.C.

Their teammates at that initial Skate Canada were the stately Canadian champions Marie-France Dubreuil and Patrice Lauzon, who had been forced to withdraw from the Olympics when Marie-France was badly injured during the competition. This season was to be their swan song in elite skating.

"They took us in and showed us the ropes," Scott says of the couple he had been gaping at in the hotel elevator at Nationals less than two years earlier. "They led by example. They were such seasoned veterans, and they helped us all year."

"We felt supported by them," Tessa continues. "And they had a reason to be threatened by us, I think. So that's why it came as a surprise in Victoria when they were so great with us. We really felt that support. And I felt it again on tour after the 2010 Olympics because we were going in as the rookies, and Marie-France and Patrice really took us in. It wasn't like they sat down and gave us advice. It was just a feeling."

Right: Attending a banquet in 2007.
Opposite: Posing on a carousel during a photoshoot.

As Tessa and Scott expected, senior competition was a different landscape than junior. Marie-France and Patrice won Skate Canada that fall — "by a mile," Scott laughs. But by earning a silver medal in their first senior Grand Prix, Tessa and Scott created a huge splash in Victoria that sent ripples of awareness across the entire ice dancing world.

Their Original Dance, skated to "Assass-ination Tango," wasn't so kind to the young Canadians in their next Grand Prix event, Trophée Eric Bompard, in Paris. They were a struggling eighth in the OD, finishing fourth overall. The French event had a much stronger field, and the top two teams there went on to win the next two world championships.

Tessa recalls thinking, as she often does, that "everyone seems so much better than us."

But Scott is Tessa's alter ego when it comes to assessing the opposition. While he may sometimes get a little over-optimistic, he always sees where the teams ahead of them were vulnerable. Tessa, on the other hand, sometimes gives the opposition too much credit. She agrees that skating fans might be surprised to learn of those doubts. "Probably," she says. "Part of what we do when we step on the ice is looking confident, looking like you think you should win. That's all part of the game. It's kind of like that duck: on the surface you're calm, but inside I was very nervous."

Scott, on the other hand, looked at the three couples above them at the French Grand Prix and decided, "We can beat these guys. I didn't think that we *should* have beaten them then. They killed us. But we weren't that far off. I thought, 'We know what we have to do in order to beat these teams.'"

Opposite: With medals at Four Continents, 2007.
Right: Performing their Original Dance program in 2007.

IN JANUARY 2007 TESSA AND SCOTT FINISHED second at Nationals, securing the world team berth that had eluded them the year before, and, after winning bronze at the Four Continents championship in Colorado Springs, headed to their first world championship in Tokyo. Tessa and Scott finished sixth, an impressive result by any standards. Their sixth-place finish was the highest world championship debut by a Canadian ice dance team in exactly forty years.

"That was huge, and we were very happy," says Tessa, who had been hoping only for a top-ten finish. "We were the very first to skate the compulsory dance and went in thinking, 'This is nice, trying to advance and move up, after the year we had the year before when we were defending, in juniors. This is a different kind of pressure: we don't have anything to lose, we can just go after it.' We had a good free skate,

sixth overall, and we were really pleased with it."

The difference between sixth and fifth, like the difference between fourth and the bronze medal, means more than just one spot. At competition, the top five couples all skate in the same flight, warm-up group, and practice session. The talent is better and the competition more fierce. And judges, being only human, have more respect and higher expectations for the final flight.

Tessa and Scott had watched the final group during the week, and immediately after leaving the kiss and cry, where they celebrated a remarkable entry onto the world stage, their first thought was all business.

"We said, 'Let's get into that last group,'" Scott says.

And that became the target for the 2007–8 season.

Above: On the street in Japan. *Opposite:* Backstage at Worlds in Tokyo.

IGURE SKATERS WORK ON THEIR NEW programs in the spring, starting with the selection of music. The designated Original Dance rhythm for 2007–8 was folk music, and Marina strongly suggested Tessa and Scott skate to the Russian gypsy piece "Dark Eyes." They liked the music, but were never truly at one with it. "We have never really related to folk music until we found that flamenco in the Olympic year," Scott explains. And Tessa recalls that all season they "took a lot of heat" from some judges who felt that the young couple from Canada didn't have the background to relate to a Russian dance. Never mind that they were being

coached every day by two Russians. But the program was popular with skating fans, and by the new year they were skating it well.

"We made it work, but it wasn't really us," Scott said.

The free dance, though, was entirely different. Marina had chosen Michel Legrand's powerful theme music from the classic, bittersweet 1964 movie *The Umbrellas of Cherbourg*. Both skaters loved it from the start. They rented the video in order to immerse themselves in their individual roles: a teenaged umbrella saleswoman and a young mechanic who fall in love. He is called away to war,

unaware she is carrying his baby, and although they promise to wait for each other, she marries another man who will support her. They never get back together.

"It was us," Tessa says. "It was two young kids kind of figuring out their love for each other. It was an interesting program for us because there was a storyline to follow. And with the lyrics, you have to get into those characters, rather than do your own interpretation."

"So we really had to pay attention to every little detail," Scott continues. "I really enjoyed playing a specific character. They were young kids when they met, so that's the part of the story we related to. We were seventeen and nineteen at the time, so it was easy for us to portray these characters because it was sort of what we were: naive kids who could fall in love."

While they were elevating their interpretive skills to keep in step with their new status as top-six in the world, Tessa and Scott were also hard at work on improving their lifts and spins.

"We knew we had the best footwork in the world but we wanted to make sure that all our elements were better than anyone else's," Scott says. "So we worked a lot on coming up with unique and difficult lifts, and when we put it all together as a package it really worked well."

"The couple of years before that, everyone had been harping on our lifts, saying they weren't intricate," Tessa says. "We were getting Level 4's [the highest level], but it was just never a focus for us."

Marina and Igor brought acrobats from a circus school in Montreal to Canton, where they worked with Tessa and Scott on basic lifting technique. While Tessa and Marina explained the impression they wanted to create and the rules

Above: A photoshoot with photographer Myra Klarman.
Opposite: Performing free dance program to the theme music from *The Umbrellas of Cherbourg*.

Above: Compulsory dance in Quebec City, 2007.
Opposite: Posing for a photo in Japan.

they had to work within, the circus performers opened the skaters' eyes to a number of new creative options. And they helped Tessa and Scott learn the circus insiders' techniques and tricks.

"Traditionally we'd thought of our lifts as really muscling them up there," Scott points out. "But we learned from them that if we worked together and counterbalanced, or if we had perfect timing and got the pop, you could make the lifts work even better than just using muscle strength on them." Working with the acrobats, they practised more off the ice than on it, and it was a turning point, Tessa says. They usually only did off-ice lifts in warm-ups at competition, assuming that the major components of the lift were the speed and momentum on the ice. Now they knew differently.

They focused mainly on the Original Dance and free dance during training, and they began adding compulsory dance practice later in the summer, at that point, however, Tessa started to feel cramps in both her shins. She'd never experienced this before and had no idea why she was in pain during compulsory dance practices, but not the OD or free dance sessions.

"So much of compulsories is sustaining a knee bend and holding an edge," she said. "I was thinking it was that or maybe my skates. I really wasn't thinking much about it, I just knew that they hurt. They didn't hurt in the OD or the free dance, so I just dealt with it."

As their competitive season opened with Skate Canada in Quebec City, Tessa was coping with the inexplicable pain by taking her skates off immediately after compulsory dance practice or competition. Tessa and Scott won by more than twenty-five points for their first senior Grand Prix victory.

"Standing on the podium was cool, but we really didn't think much of it," Scott says. "We just

wanted to go there and skate well, and get the programs underneath us. Our goal was to make the Grand Prix Final in Torino."

Which they did by finishing second at the NHK Trophy competition in Japan a couple of weeks later. Tessa's legs had hurt during the compulsories, and perhaps that's why she sometimes felt that they were overmatched in the competition, despite the fact that they won two of the three segments. No matter how she was feeling inside, they were proving now on a regular basis that they

could skate with the world's best. They could, but at the Grand Prix Final in Torino, they didn't, finishing fourth overall. The Final, as it's known in skaters' parlance, includes only the Original Dance and a free dance. Scott made a major mistake on the twizzle sequence in the OD and they never fully recovered. The free dance, which they had trained for longer and had felt more comfortable with from the start, was strong.

The team and their coaches were discouraged because they had hoped to use The Final as a springboard to a strong showing at Worlds. But they learned that year that it's not as important to win The Final as it is draw something positive out of it, something to work on before the bigger event three months later.

What Scott drew out of missing the podium at the Grand Prix Final was that, despite their finish, he saw that he and Tessa were as good as, or even better than, everybody else. "We should beat them," he thought. And that's one of the key differences in their emotional makeup. "I did NOT think that," Tessa says emphatically. "I tell her we're the best every practice," Scott says.

"Which is good," Tessa finishes, "because I'm sitting there getting a bit frightened, thinking, 'We don't even deserve to be here.'"

Scott admits, though, that at The Final he got so excited at the prospect of being the best that he tried to hurry the process rather than taking it a day at a time, "and letting the training speak for itself, the skating speak for itself." It was an important lesson.

Tessa, too, was going through some self-discovery at the time. While Scott got along with the male skaters, despite finding the dressing room far too silent before a competition, Tessa had been taking it personally when the female skaters wouldn't talk to her, or were outright rude to her, in the dressing room. She didn't recognize that it was all part of the high-octane competitive atmosphere.

"I want to please and I want people to like me," she explains, "but that was *the* season that I started to realize that I couldn't worry about other people and I had to be okay with going in and being in a bubble." Again, it was a lesson, which would pay off in the future.

So while Scott's competitive confidence was a boost to Tessa's competition-week doubts (for the first eight or nine years she was sick at every competition, sometimes right on the ice, then felt fine and confident), those same doubts fuelled her determination to figure out ways to get better. She brought structure and planning to Scott's enthusiasm and bravado.

The second-year seniors expected to win the Canadian championships, held in January at the Pacific Coliseum in Vancouver, and used it as a

> "I WANT TO PLEASE AND I WANT PEOPLE TO LIKE ME, BUT THAT WAS THE SEASON THAT I STARTED TO REALIZE THAT I COULDN'T WORRY ABOUT OTHER PEOPLE AND I HAD TO BE OKAY WITH GOING IN AND BEING IN A BUBBLE." —*Tessa*

virtual tune-up for the Four Continents competition and Worlds. It was more of a coronation than a competition, and they beat the silver medallists by nearly thirty-five points.

In a bit of a role reversal, Tessa was the one who was envisioning victory over the best couples in the world in Vancouver: "I said to Scott many times, 'This is our rink. We're going to win Nationals here and then we're going to the Olympics.'"

But the Olympics were twenty-four months away, while Four Continents was the next hurdle. They won their first Four Continents competition, defeating Meryl Davis and Charlie White handily. Marina, who coaches both pairs, used a variety of psychological tricks and coaching techniques, as she always has done in the name of teaching her students to flourish under varied circumstances. For instance, she floods the rink surface only twice in the twelve-hour day at Canton, which helps dancers deal with poor ice conditions, especially in the latter, rutted rounds of compulsories. And while

Above: Performing the compulsory dance
during the NHK Trophy in Japan, 2007.
Opposite: A break during a photoshoot
for *Hello! Canada* magazine.

Tessa and Scott didn't skate well at The Final, Marina felt that at least Scott had learned not to get over-excited when he feels confident. And at Four Continents and Nationals, knowing that Tessa and Scott weren't in much danger of losing, she started to mess with their minds, trying to get them ready for any kind of disruption.

When Tessa and Scott began using key words at that competition, saying, "Let's really enjoy this spot," she'd interrupt, agitated, and say "NO!", implying that they really had to push through that segment of the program. She was simply trying to throw them off their game because, as she repeatedly said, "You have to learn to compete under any conditions."

Tessa and Scott had no idea what conditions would be like for them at their second Worlds, in Gothenburg, Sweden. They'd had an excellent debut at sixth the previous year, but they were hoping there would be no repeat of the Grand Prix Final.

"We were thinking we weren't at our best and we finished fourth at Final, so let's skate our best and skate for a medal," Tessa recalls. "Just our second year and we're fighting for a medal."

Scott thought they were as good as any of the

Opposite: Performing the free dance at Four Continents, 2008.
Top: Gold medal win at Four Continents.
Bottom: With coach Marina Zoueva.

top teams, but there was Tessa's nagging shin problem, which was compounded by the fact that practices for the original dance and compulsories, the pain-causing culprit, were held together. That meant entire practices of agony until the compulsories were over. A month earlier, Tessa had started working with physiotherapist Mary Brannagan in Tecumseh, a suburb of Windsor. She treated Tessa's shins with fascial release techniques which diminished the pain. But the effects of the treatment did not last. "As soon as I skated I would be in agony again." Tessa says.

"The compulsory pattern was the Argentine Tango, and after the first half pattern they would start to burn," she recalls. "I told someone in my family, 'Just so you know when you're watching me skate: after the first half I'm dying and there's another round and a half to go.'"

But Tessa's skating, and her face, didn't betray the pain she was enduring, and they delivered an excellent Argentine, finishing a shocking second to the French team.

After an exemplary compulsory, Tessa and Scott also turned in a terrific Original Dance until the dying seconds, when she did one too few rotations in the twizzles. They were hit hard by the judges and dropped to third.

"We'd learned from The Final that we needed to go out and do what we do at home, not get too excited," Tessa said. "It was a great skate until the end and I was so mad at myself afterwards. I felt guilty, I kind of felt like I let the team down. But Scott's so good about that."

"We know it's a team," Scott replies. "I could easily have lost count on my twizzles too. We don't get mad at each other, it doesn't make sense. You do a good skate together, you do a bad skate together. I think in ice dance that applies more than in any other discipline because you're always holding on, always touching each other."

"We hear teams yelling and swearing at each other all the time," Tessa says. "We've never said so much as 'shut up' to one another. We have such great respect for each other, and I think because we never started down that path of blaming or name-calling, we didn't get into the pattern."

Tessa and Scott were determined to regain the spot they had dropped with the OD, and armed with a free dance they'd loved since they heard the opening notes, they did exactly that. It was the best they ever skated "Umbrellas."

"It didn't even feel like we were skating out there," Scott recalls. "Usually we have to work really hard in that free dance, but it started and the next second it was over. I always chase that feeling."

Opposite: Original Dance at Worlds in Sweden.
Left: (top) During practice, *(bottom)* a break after competition.

"It didn't even feel like we were skating out there. Usually we have to work really hard in that free dance, but it started and the next second it was over. I always chase that feeling."—*Scott*

They were so excited with how they had skated under pressure that they bounced around the kiss and cry and weren't concerned about the actual placement. "Then it came up on the big screen and we could actually see the Ordinal '1' for free dance," Tessa said. "It was the coolest. We hugged each other for the longest time."

The memory of which makes Scott laugh warmly: "When Tessa gets really excited, she does this thing between a laugh and a cry. It's the best. Usually I'm hugging her at that point and it's so awesome. That was the first hug-laugh, I remember. She was just so happy."

And Igor turned to them and said, "You won the free dance! You're free dance world champions."

"Standing on the podium, we were excited to be world silver medallists, but I didn't associate it with being second in the world," Scott recalls. "I thought, 'Oh *yeah*, this is the biggest competition of the year, and we rocked it. We could at least sense that we could be the best. I remember saying to my mom, 'I never want to lose a competition ever again.'"

With the silver medal — and with the un-scripted light brush-kiss at the end of the free dance, their first on-ice contact of that kind of intimacy — all of Canada seemed to suddenly discover Tessa Virtue and Scott Moir. Canadians put them on their Olympic radar and many of them assumed that they were a romantic couple. The dancers themselves consider that a compliment because it means they're selling their programs well.

"I understand," Tessa smiles, "because when I see movies I'm feeling, 'Oh, but they should be together!'"

Their impressive surge to the silver medal marked the first time in forty-seven years that

Canadian ice dancers had medalled as early as their second Worlds, and Tessa and Scott felt they were perfectly positioned for the Olympics. They were the best free dancers in the world, but didn't have to hang onto a world title for the better part of two years. They were hoping, bordering on believing, that they'd win the 2009 Worlds, come into Vancouver on a roll, and win the Olympics.

"We were on track," Tessa says. "We knew we needed to work hard that fall to be the best."

But as Tessa's shins would angrily remind her, sometimes you can work *too* hard.

Just one step removed from the top of the podium, Tessa and Scott knew they could be world champions in 2009, and, by extension, Olympic champions in 2010. They'd often use "Best in the World" as their key words in practice. That motivated them to a training intensity they'd never reached before. "In retrospect," Tessa smiles, "we got a little bit crazy, I think. We wanted it so badly. Marina and Igor wanted it so badly. We knew the next step was winning."

Opposite: Performing compulsory dance during Worlds, 2008. *Above:* Tessa and Scott on their way to a charity dinner.

"WE WERE ON TRACK, WE KNEW WE NEEDED
TO WORK HARD THAT FALL TO BE THE BEST." —*Tessa*

They started spending between ten and thirteen hours per day at the Canton rink, with as many as eight of those hours on the ice. Tessa was also lifting weights and working out five days a week. She put on five pounds of muscle and lost two pounds of fat in four weeks. Scott was spending more time than previously in off-ice dance sessions and training at the barre. They had, in essence, doubled their training from any other summer and were happy to do so, but they were overdoing it.

"We felt every fourteen-hour day makes you a world champion,'" Scott explains.

The couple spent hours and hours together off the ice, working again with the acrobats from Montreal and experimenting on their own with new lifts and positions. They had decided to institute new lifts for the 2008–9 season, with as much innovation and degree of difficulty as they could. Normally they would have recycled from previous programs at least some of the three lifts, plus a creative lift (with no level attached to it) required for the free dance.

With that in mind, one morning that summer Marina brought a ballet magazine into the arena and flipped it open to a picture of a ballerina, arms spread, balanced on one knee on the back of her partner, who was bent over in a squat position. None of them had any idea at the time that this was the beginning of one of the most memorable moves in Canadian ice dancing history.

"She said, 'I think you can do this,'" Tessa recalls. "We were thinking 'You're crazy, that's never going to happen.' We really couldn't see how the mechanics of it worked, where her weight was centred. We tried it off the ice, and it was hard."

"And on the ice, it was scary," says Scott.

In the illustration, the man's feet were pointed straight ahead, where Scott's would have to be splayed sideways so he could glide. It was hard to simulate off ice because they didn't have the momentum they would on ice. They also had to find the right position for Tessa to step up onto Scott's back, and make sure she didn't cut him. They had to work out whether she was going to

Above left: An informal training session.
Above right: At the rink in Canton, Michigan.
Opposite: "The Goose"

enter the lift skating forwards or backwards, how far Scott would bend over, how much weight she could exert with her right skate, which would be in Scott's thigh, and how much pressure her right knee could exert on his back.

It took several exasperating months, but they finally found a workable version of the lift people had started calling the Eagle, because Tessa looked as if she were flying. But that sounded too American for a Canadian couple, so they eventually renamed it The Goose, in honour of one of Canada's national symbols.

Marina told them later that she never thought they would get it, but she wasn't taking

into account the very nature of their partnership: they are competitive about everything and they never give up. And how early in their careers in Kitchener-Waterloo, they had often been challenged to attempt hyper-difficult moves.

"The other part was that we knew we had something different, which is hard to find with the rules," Scott explains. "And we needed to get it in order to be different."

They inserted The Goose into their new free dance, which was skated to two songs by Pink Floyd, a drastic departure for them. They knew that in the following year, the Olympic season,

they'd be returning to their forte — something more classical and romantic — and wanted to show that they could skate to a variety of musical genres.

"Pink Floyd took us in another direction, but we also needed to set ourselves up to win," Tessa said. "So it was the balance of 'how hard do we push it this year without playing it safe, but still put ourselves in gold medal position?'"

Tessa and Scott loved the Pink Floyd program, but were never able to skate it to its full potential. Because of all the summer skating and off-ice work, both of Tessa's shins were quickly turning into ovens of pain.

They only practised sections of their compulsory dances, thinking that was the source of Tessa's severe leg cramping. But as the summer progressed, so did the pain, no matter what kind of skating they were doing, which she could endure for even shorter periods. "I always felt like I had to take my skates off," Tessa says, wincing at the memory. "The anterior muscle, which runs along the shin bone, was on fire. By September we couldn't make it through the programs. I could skate for maybe thirty seconds and I would have to stop: my legs would cramp, give out, and I'd lose feeling down into my feet. I'd have drop-foot, where your foot kind of just clumps because your shin doesn't work."

At first doctors thought it was shin splints, but they eventually ruled that out. Stress fractures were also ruled out. Over the summer Tessa visited four doctors. Some suggested rest; others suggested pushing through the pain. Tessa followed every suggestion but the pain just kept getting worse. So Tessa and Scott were getting frustrated and a little anxious.

"I would skate for thirty seconds and then it looked from the outside like I'd give up," says

Above: (left to right), Tessa, Joannie Rochette, Miki Ando, and Mao Asada.
Opposite: Tessa and Scott share a quiet moment on the ice during Nationals in 2009.

Tessa, the woman who never gives up. "This is the year we're supposed to be winning everything, setting ourselves up to be Olympic champions. This is the year for us and we can't even make it through a minute of our program."

While they were doing small segments of programs, as much as Tessa could stand, they weren't letting anyone, even their training mates in Canton, know the depth of her severe pain. For one thing, they didn't know what it was, and, for another, if judges found out about the injury, there was a chance they would expect a lower level of skating, which could affect the neutrality of their judging.

"They look for you to be weak rather than look for you to be strong," Scott explains.

Finally, just before they left for a national team training camp in Vancouver in September, Tessa was tested for chronic exertional compartment syndrome, a condition related to muscle overuse. A few days later, the results came back positive.

"The problem was that the tissue around my muscle was tight and the muscles couldn't expand when I exerted myself," Tessa explains. "Then the blood flow is limited and all the waste and toxins are stuck in there."

Tessa visited Skate Canada's Dr. Julia Alleyne, who explained that her options were to have surgery, which might or might not work, or to retire, something Tessa wouldn't dream of. So surgery it was.

"The surgery idea was kind of good news," says Tessa, who could barely walk by then. "Part of me was happy that something could be done about it. The other part of me was already starting to calculate, 'How long before I can get back?' The injury isn't that uncommon, but doctors don't know that much about it. And every case is different. After I talked to Dr. Julia, I had a little moment of crying. Then I called Scott, and then Marina and Igor."

"We all felt the same way," Scott continues. "At least we knew. It was weird that nobody knew what it was for so long."

On October 2, 2008, Dr. Kevin Willits of London's world-famous Fowler Kennedy Sport Medicine Clinic performed the four-hour surgery. He made a two pairs of two-inch vertical — not circular as widely reported — incisions in each leg about four inches below the knee, and cut through the tissue around Tessa's shin muscle so the muscle had room to expand and contract. Over time, the scars healed astonishingly well, although she does have a slight bulging above the ankle on both legs

Tessa recuperated at home in London, under strong pain medication, and says she lost "all my muscle" within two weeks.

She and Scott knew they'd be missing their first Grand Prix assignment, Skate Canada, but hoped they would be ready to compete for the NHK Trophy in November. But every compartment syndrome case is different, and there hadn't

Opposite: Compulsory dance at Four Continents in Vancouver, 2009.
Left: With coaches Igor Shpilband and Marina Zoueva.

been many examples to draw upon. It turned out Tessa wasn't able to get back on skates for two full months. She required intense physiotherapy to build up her strength and to learn how to walk again. She had to increase her physical activity gradually, which was difficult emotionally because she wanted to jump right back into high-level training.

Scott, meanwhile, was in Canton, running through their programs on the ice by himself and working harder in the gym than he ever had. They were hoping Tessa would be ready for NHK, but when that deadline came and went he worried that they might also miss the National championships in early January.

In early December Scott met Tessa at London's Kinsmen Arena for her "first baby steps" on the ice. She was able to skate for only about ten minutes, "kind of walking at first. I felt like a CanSkate [beginner] skater."

Preferring to avoid the scrutiny in Canton, they remained in London for another two weeks, adding a couple of minutes of skating every day, basically just holding hands and stroking together around the ice. When they returned to their Michigan training base, they were up to half an hour of stroking per day, but hadn't practised any segments of their programs. And Nationals were just three weeks away.

But the worst development was something only they knew about, and their voices still crack when they try to describe it.

"We didn't talk," they say, in perfect unison.

Much is made of how long Tessa and Scott have been together, but the corollary is just how little of their lives they've spent apart. They've known each other since they were six and eight, teamed up at eight and ten years old, and for years had spent eight hours or more per day together with only two weeks off per year. They didn't know any other situation except "together."

But during Tessa's recovery time — the longest they'd ever spent apart — they weren't in regular communication with each other. It was complicated but, essentially, they were protecting each other: she didn't want to unload her troubles on him, and he didn't want to rub it in that he was on the ice every day. When they got back together, though, they realized they'd made a horrible mistake.

"That was the worst time for our relationship, and unfortunately it was matched up with the worst time of our skating career," Tessa says, wincing. "For twelve years, we didn't even have to form full sentences to understand each other. And then we spent all that time apart and we weren't even talking."

"It was like we grew apart so much in those two months," Scott adds. "That was a whole part of it that we didn't expect. We had to learn how to get along and try to support each other. It was really quite strange."

Tessa had to quickly relearn the programs, now more fully evolved, while Scott also had to make adjustments. Skating alone, he had turned some of the segments into virtual solos, and he had to relearn them with a partner beside him. And there were constant disappointments, because a good training day would give them optimism that Tessa's leg problems were over, then "the very next day I'd be crying at the boards because I couldn't do anything with the pain."

Opposite: Performing the Viennese Waltz during compulsory dance at Canadian championships.

In January, Tessa had started seeing Mary Brannagan again for post-operative physiotherapy, which emphasized fascial release and deep leg massage. She would continue regular treatment right through the Olympic season, including the two weeks of the Vancouver Games. For the first few months the massage therapy treatments were quite painful, the worst part being when Mary worked through the scar tissues.

"And I also had to deal with the persistent numbness between the scars," Tessa recalls with a grimace. "The most frustrating part was feeling better after the treatments with Mary and then walking for five minutes and feeling pain or, worse, skating for just two minutes, feeling unbearable pain and having to stop."

They trained the programs in segments, and in a period when they'd normally be doing two run-throughs per day, they managed only one complete run-through before the Canadian championships. And the next day Tessa was in so much pain she couldn't walk.

The compulsory dance for the Canadian championships was the Viennese Waltz, of which they had done just one pass all year. Essentially, their entire training for it consisted of the five-minute warm-up at Nationals.

"We were just trying to get through it without embarrassing ourselves," Tessa says. "I felt sick about it."

But they did get through it, and also their demanding quick Original Dance. They had become realistic about their difficult Pink Floyd free dance — "We loved that program," Scott says — and removed a few interesting steps to make it easier on Tessa's legs. They won the competition without severe challenge, an important step in their recovery process, but the cost was more than a week of lost training in order for Tessa's shins to fully recover. They weren't able to train much before heading to Four Continents in Vancouver, where they were to face Meryl Davis and Charlie White, who'd been enjoying a breakthrough season.

In hindsight, Tessa and Scott had had almost no training, and so shouldn't have worried about their actual results for the rest of the season. But they are ultra-competitive, and had convinced themselves they needed to win because they were ranked second in the world and because Four Continents would set a tone for how they felt about the Pacific Coliseum, where the Olympics would be held a year later. They got through the relatively easy Finn Step compulsory, weren't in good enough physical shape to really push their Original Dance program but still won the segment, then lost the free dance, and the gold medal, to Meryl and Charlie.

"Looking back, we were just lucky and happy to make it to the end, really," Scott recalls. "When we started the last part, which is supposed to be the part with the most energy and the most excitement, we were just dog-tired My skates were stuck to the ice, and I couldn't move. We were doing what we call July run-throughs with 8,000 people there."

Tessa felt that they were letting people down with their performances, and also a bit guilty that she was saying to the public that she felt great when in reality she was experiencing great pain most days.

"We didn't want to lie," she explains. "But we needed to say that everything was fine to believe and to be able to step on the ice and actually compete. Part of it was that, unfortunately, kind of like in the NHL, you don't say you're injured because they [the judges] come after you and we already had enough going against us."

Competing at Four Continents cost them another week of hard training for the Worlds, which were held in Los Angeles, but, ever optimistic, they felt they could still win. Their Paso Doble compulsories were strong, even though they hadn't made it through the necessary three patterns in one try, and they had immense confidence in their Pink Floyd free dance. At Worlds, they skated better compulsories than they had the previous two competitions and were third, despite Tessa "dying" after the first pattern. In the Original Dance, Scott "mucked up the twizzles ten seconds in," and they "were pretty shaky for the rest of the program." Ironically, the twizzles are individual elements, the only ones he could effectively practise on his own while Tessa was in post-op recovery in London.

They went on to skate their free dance "as well as we could under the circumstances," and had just enough to hang on to the bronze medal.

110 | ROAD TO GOLD

"WE LOOKED BACK AND SAID, 'WOW, WHAT A YEAR.'"—*Scott*

While they weren't happy with getting only a bronze, Scott says, "We looked back and said, 'Wow, what a year.'" And those closest to them, including Igor, felt that finishing third with their minimal, unfamiliar training patterns and with Tessa enduring such pain may have been their greatest achievement yet. Although they were still confident about the Olympics, they also had some deep apprehension because, while they had been told that Tessa should be recovered by Christmas, the season was already over and she was still experiencing pain after heavy training.

And they had a great deal of repair work to do on their relationship, which they'd put off because they had so much to do just to get their on-ice product in passable shape. They were getting along well on the ice, but were still virtual strangers off it. And that was eating away at both of them.

They did not "have a comfort zone unless we were on the ice," recalls Scott. "We were scared out of our minds that our Olympic dream was not going to be realized because of it." If they hadn't had such a history of togetherness, he says, they wouldn't have managed to skate at all in 2008–9. "So that off-season we spent a lot of time just trying to get back together, trying to become the friends that we had always been."

Friends who would go to the Olympics — and win them — just like they'd always planned.

Right: Presenting gifts at a ceremony. *Below:* Performing Pink Floyd free dance program at Worlds, 2009.

"When I picked that music, I knew somehow that they would win. I knew it had total harmony for them. Every day in July 2009, I had them finish their program standing facing the Canadian flag in our rink in Canton, hands on their hearts. I know how  patriotic they are. What they did, they did not do for themselves but for Canada." —*Marina Zoueva*

Chapter Five

TRIUMPH ON ICE

"We felt so proud to be Canadian and to be part of these Games." —*Scott*

To elite athletes nothing is more thrilling, or more pressure-packed, than an Olympics in their own country. The Winter Games always offer the potential for glory and also the burden of expectation, but both are multiplied many times over when your country is the host nation.

Tessa and Scott began thinking constantly about the Vancouver Olympics in June 2009, with the date February 22, 2010 — the night of the free dance final — etched permanently in their minds. From midsummer onward, there were increasingly energized references to Vancouver 2010.

Tessa and Scott had won a world bronze medal despite their lack of training depth, her frequent debilitating pain, and the sudden disappearance of their unique off-ice closeness. To outsiders things seemed to be back on track; only the skaters knew that their joined-at-the-hip friendship wasn't quite back yet, and that Tessa's shins were still getting in the way of Olympic-level training.

"I knew I had support from Scott and he had it from me, but we weren't expressing that," Tessa says. "Because we didn't know how to."

They had never needed to know how because it had always come so naturally. Recognizing this, each of them began working with sports psychologists in the off-season. It was something that they had already planned to do in the Olympic season anyway, to help them organize and focus their thoughts amid all the domestic hype and pressure.

"I needed to relearn how to communicate with my partner," explains Scott, who had been trained by Suzanne Killing early in his career to analyze the team's needs. "I couldn't understand why I couldn't communicate with my partner." It would take much of the Olympic season for Tessa and Scott to restore, and then tighten even more, their longtime closeness and off-ice friendship. Outsiders, who had always assumed it was so easy for the couple to communicate, had no idea of how much of an emotional toll this was taking on both skaters. That stress was increased more by the fact that the after-effects of surgery were not abating very quickly: in fact they continued all season.

Tessa really ramped up her physiotherapy during the summer of 2009 driving the one hour from Canton to Tecumseh four or five times per week for two-hour sessions. The physiotherapy was

Opposite: "The Goose" at the Grand Prix Final in Tokyo, Japan, 2009.

no longer painful but it was frustrating that the recuperative effects wouldn't last long. All season, Tessa dealt with constant disappointment: "I was either in too much pain to skate or I would feel better, push myself and end up having a major setback."

There was not one competition, nor one training day, during the entire Olympic season when Tessa was completely physically healthy. Amidst the emotional upheaval and constant pain, Tessa sometimes lost confidence in her skating, and truly believed that other skaters were laughing at her in training. She had to work very hard to overcome those severe self-doubts.

able to tell her if we didn't like it? We decided, okay, it's our Olympics, we have to tell her."

One morning Marina grabbed her car keys and said, "Follow me. It's time." So all three of them put their skate guards on, clomped through the arena parking lot, and sat in Marina's car. She played a segment of Gustav Mahler's Symphony no. 5, a textured classical work that is both big and subtle at the same time. Very few skaters have used it because of its elusive, almost ghostly quality, one that can be mistaken for sombreness instead of the uplifting themes Marina and her skaters heard.

"When I listened to it, I loved it," Scott said,

> "…I LOVED IT. IT WAS ETHEREAL, WITH THE PIANO, THE VIOLINS, AND THE WHOLE ORCHESTRA. THERE ARE SO MANY LITTLE CLIMAXES. I THOUGHT THERE WERE SO MANY GOOD MOMENTS WHEN IT JUST BUILDS. I KEPT THINKING TO MYSELF, 'THIS IS OUR OLYMPIC MOMENT.'"—*Tessa*

Meanwhile, Igor was impressed by how she and her partner were handling their off-ice emotional estrangement. "They kept it so professional on the ice," he said. "I didn't see it affect them on the ice. The way they treated the injury and what they did the year before, they deserved a medal for that. In my experience I haven't known of any other team who could do what they did with the training they had."

Like all Canadian medal contenders, Tessa and Scott wanted to make sure that they did everything possible to help their game rise to the massive domestic expectations. For figure skaters, this included choosing musical accompaniment that was memorable, and as close to perfect as possible.

Tessa and Scott knew that Marina had a long-term plan for their Olympic music, but Marina wasn't letting on what it was. They were getting anxious because the Olympic pressure was already closing in, but they didn't know what musical vehicle they'd be using to combat it. "We actually talked about what we were going to say to her if we didn't like it," Scott reveals. "Would we be

"And I kept thinking, 'I hope Tessa likes it, I really hope Tessa likes it.'"

No worry, Tessa recalls, "because ten notes in, I loved it. It was ethereal, with the piano, the violins, and the whole orchestra. There are so many little climaxes. I thought there were so many good moments when it just builds. I kept thinking to myself, 'This is our Olympic moment.'"

"We walked back into the rink," Scott continues, "and said, 'Yes.'"

And that was one of the major steps toward regaining their off-ice relationship: they were thinking the same way again and they were playing off of each other's excitement. Although they had no idea what the exact choreography would be — it was the first time in her career that Tessa did not immediately plan where specific elements should go in the music — they were each already visualizing skating to Mahler in Vancouver. The work was pulling them together as it had already started to do, without them really knowing it, during the previous year's struggles.

And Marina and Igor were including their

Opposite: Tessa and Scott during practice at the Skate Canada training camp, 2009.

students in the creative process more than they ever had, which also helped unite them in a common purpose. "They would say, 'We want you to get from here to here, what do *you* feel comfortable doing?'" Tessa recalls. "And we'd come up with something and they'd make it better. So things really came from us. I mean, Marina had this vision, but the actual steps came from us, because it was just natural."

"It was *our* program," Scott says. "It's us. We made it, we helped Marina make it. She really took our greatest strengths and put them into the program."

With Igor working out the footwork and transitions, Scott listening repeatedly to the Mahler piece on his weekend drives back to Ilderton, and all four of them envisioning the same end result and contributing to the choreography, the Olympic free dance came together by July 1. Canada Day, fittingly. It was the quickest they'd ever assembled a program, which gave them more time to practise it.

The development of their Original Dance, however, was proceeding at a snail's pace. The rhythm for 2009–10 was folk dance, as it had been two years earlier, and the ISU expected that most teams would select music from their own country. Which is exactly what Tessa and Scott hoped to do.

But after listening to countless cuts of Canadian music and consulting with music experts, they came up dry. Nothing they heard seemed to have an Olympic-sized dimension to it. Stymied, they began searching elsewhere. They were looking for something strong and powerful to go with the beauty and grace of Mahler. After the skaters rejected Marina's suggestion of Mexican music, Tessa mentioned "maybe Spanish" and Marina soon handed them a stack of twenty-five flamenco CDs. Of all the cuts, they found just one song they liked: "Farrucas," by Pepe Romero.

Tessa and Scott correctly assumed that Marina wasn't sold on the flamenco, and they weren't sure themselves that it was going to work. But they loved the music, and when they applied the previous year's footwork to it, they found it was also fun to skate to: an important consideration when they would have to hear it hundreds of times before the Olympics.

To capture the feel of the flamenco, they worked with dancers who had lived and trained in Spain, and later with Chicago-based Luis Montero, one of the world's most respected Spanish dancers. But so much of what the flamenco dancers did was not transferable to the ice because they were working on a stage not much bigger than a dinner table. Tessa and Scott had so much speed and flow

Opposite: Performing the flamenco in November 2009. *Right:* Practising footwork.

on the ice that they couldn't do many of the positions they were being shown. But they kept cobbling it together, regularly removing some segments and adding others.

Much of the pre-Olympic summer they focused on the free dance, and were able to do full run-throughs because Tessa's shins weren't plaguing her too much. She thought the pain had vanished for good, but when they started working Original Dance practices into their training regimen, and doing back-to-back programs, her shins got bad again. At the national team test camp in Vancouver in September, she couldn't make it through the free dance.

"We were almost a year out of surgery and a few months away from competing in the Olympic Games and I can't get through a program," Tessa recalls. "I just lost it after that. I was crying and in pain."

"Other athletes would try to comfort us," Scott recalls, "and we would say, '*get away* from us.'"

They weren't able to train much before their first Grand Prix in Paris, and although they felt on top of their free dance, their Original Dance felt sloppy because of all the new additions. But after getting over their frustration, they gradually devised an alternative training plan. They would do a thirty-second part of their program, then take a thirty-second break, then do a ten-second part and take a short break. It was a form of interval training, and it helped build endurance into Tessa's legs. They couldn't manage full run-throughs, but at least every segment of the programs was practised.

"So when we had to do a full run-through at competition we could make it because everything was trained," Scott said. "It was completely different for us."

Under normal circumstances Tessa and Scott would have a four-week schedule before competition doing back-to-back run-throughs, with only a five-minute rest, every day for a week, then follow with a week of easier training. Then they'd repeat the cycle. Four months out from the Games,

Right: Leaving the ice after a session at Skate Canada training camp in Vancouver, B.C., September 2009.

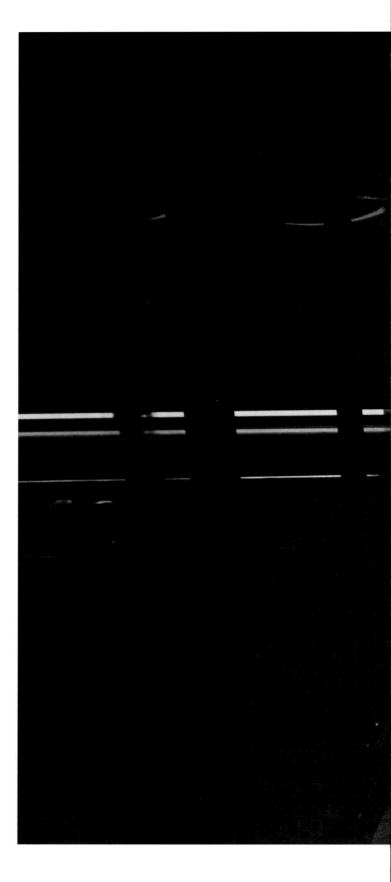

however, they were doing three run-throughs in a week at most, although the interval training was really helping.

But as Kate Virtue was driving her daughter to the airport for the flight to the Grand Prix in Paris, Tessa began crying uncontrollably, and said her legs were hurting so badly she probably couldn't make it through the programs.

"Why are we going, then? Why are we doing this?" Kate asked.

"Because I have to get to the Olympics!" Tessa answered.

At Trophée Eric Bompard, the compulsories and OD are combined into a single day, which Tessa knew would be the hardest challenge she would face all season. They hadn't yet completed a run-through of the Golden Waltz, the difficult compulsory selection, but had become accustomed to competing without enough training, so the compulsories went well. They were also determined to skate well in practice sessions so that judges in attendance would be prepared to award them the scores between nine and ten points they'd need in components to win the Games. They won all three segments in Paris to capture their first Grand Prix in nearly two years, and Tessa came away knowing that while there was still pain, she could manage three programs in two days, boosting her confidence.

Enjoying their free dance immensely and pulling on the same oar to get their OD in shape, Tessa and Scott were as unified on the ice as they'd ever been. It was spilling over into their off-ice relationship, but that was still very much a work in progress. They weren't really getting along off the ice and weren't talking to each other, outside of skating-related discussions. There is always pressure on ice dancers to be seen together away from the rink in order to create the impression that they're a true, inseparable partnership. That pressure became particularly evident to Tessa and Scott once they reached senior ranks.

"We had people say to us, 'Go be seen. Go eat together, because people are watching,'" Tessa says.

"But we *are* together," Scott continues, "so we don't have to fake it."

However, a year after her surgery, Tessa and Scott still weren't together the way they had been since the early days of their partnership, and it was eating at both of them. Tessa explains that they had somehow lost the deep trust in each other they had built through so many years, and it was taking a long time to recover it. They recall that at the Paris Grand Prix they felt the pressure to be seen together greater than they ever had, likely because they did not *feel* together.

Tessa also had an effective sounding board in her physiotherapist, Mary Brannagan, who spent six hours a day in Paris working on her legs. That was financed by B2ten, a private sector program that supports Canadian Olympians, and Scott and Tessa were quick to thank that organization in media interviews during the Games. Mary "became the place I could go to talk and vent and feel comfortable. I could talk through my program with her and she had me feeling confident," Tessa says, thankfully.

In their first Grand Prix of the season, all skaters collect indirect feedback from international judges, and what the Canadians were hearing was that their free dance was impressive but that the OD needed more polishing and more character and authenticity. Before Skate Canada, five weeks later, they worked with Luis Montero again to elevate their flamenco to the next level. They could do only a light week of training after Paris so Tessa's legs could recover, but they had been expecting that. They shifted into a higher gear, still not at the training intensity they'd been at most of their careers but no longer limited to two or three program run-throughs per week.

For the Olympic season only, Skate Canada had been moved to the sixth and final spot on the Grand Prix calendar, just two weeks from The Final. It was at The Aud in Kitchener. "Most of our friends were there, and we were feeling pretty good and raring to go," Scott recalls.

The compulsory dance, "Tango Romantica," was easier on Tessa's shins than the Golden Waltz, but they hadn't done a full pattern of it until they arrived in Kitchener, and did only one run-through there in practice. But, as in Paris, they pulled it out and won the segment. They also won the OD, but Tessa "wasn't mentally in it" and stumbled three

"WE WERE TICKED OFF BECAUSE WE DIDN'T SKATE WELL,
BUT WE WERE MORE DISAPPOINTED BECAUSE WE HAD
SO MANY PEOPLE IN THE CROWD AND WANTED TO SKATE WELL
FOR THEM. WE TALKED ABOUT IT AND SAID, 'LET'S JUST
DO WELL IN THE FREE DANCE TOMORROW.'" —*Scott*

times. She says part of the problem was that in looking around the rink for friends and relatives before they skated — something she had always done, but not since her surgery — she lost focus. Scott also made a mistake in the twizzle. "That was probably the first time we had a disaster and were composed about it," Scott says. "We were ticked off because we didn't skate well, but we were more disappointed because we had so many people in the

crowd and wanted to skate well for them. We talked about it and said, 'Let's just do well in the free dance tomorrow.'"

"Looking back, it was the perfect thing that could have happened to us," Tessa now says. "We needed to learn to compete under different circumstances."

"And we knew we needed to change some of that OD too," Scott says, which they eventually did.

Above: Tessa and Scott listen as their marks are posted during the Skate Canada competition, 2009.

Above: Tessa with her brother Casey outside of Bob Evans restaurant. *Left*:The end of their free dance program at Nationals, January 2010.

"The next day we went out and did a beautiful free dance, and we really captured the moment. We felt like the competition was a triumph because we'd come back and really skated well. It could have been a disaster."

Instead, it was a pivotal moment in their Olympic year. Tessa had been so distressed by her stumbles in the OD that she had trouble raising the enthusiasm for the free dance. But warming up off-ice "something just clicked," and she went to the right place mentally, convinced she had to stay in a personal bubble during the rest of the year's competitions. They skated brilliantly to win by nineteen points, and one judge even gave them a ten for performance, the first ever for ice dancers under the new system.

"That was a big turning point in the off-ice relationship," Tessa now realizes. "We had to be supportive and we had to be there for each other."

Tessa was still in regular pain from her shins, but with Scott's and Mary Brannagan's help she had learned to manage her injury so that it wasn't a distraction and didn't affect her performance.

With their first two-win season on the Grand Prix, Tessa and Scott headed to December's Grand Prix Final in Tokyo feeling buoyed. Their main opposition there would be their training mates Meryl Davis and Charlie White, who had also won twice that fall and whose Bollywood-themed Original Dance was considered the best in the world that autumn. Tessa and Scott's plane from Detroit was delayed on the tarmac for five hours and eventually grounded. By the time they made it to Japan, it was the night before the Original Dance. In the opening segment, they hit a wall of fatigue partway through, but performed decently.

"We were fine with it — well, not fine, exactly, because we're so competitive — but Meryl and Charlie's OD was *the* OD of the season," Tessa says. "That was their program, where the free dance felt more like our program."

Posing for a photo following the Grand Prix Final in Tokyo, Japan. *From left*, Bronze medallists Nathalie Pechalat and Fabian Bourzat of France; gold medallists Meryl Davis and Charlie White of the U.S., and silver medallists Tessa and Scott.

Scott, meanwhile, liked the idea that with their win Meryl and Charlie might be the team other couples would be gunning for at the Olympics, "and we would be kind of lying in the weeds."

At The Final, the Canadians had gotten wind that many judges were starting to consider their signature lift, The Goose, illegal. It had a rotation and a quarter in Tessa's exit, rather than the limit of one turn, even though it was when she was dismounting rather than being lifted. "We looked for answers," Scott said, "because as far as we were concerned we weren't going to the Olympics to get second."

Together, they chomped at the bit to leave Japan and get back to Canton to redesign the exit

"where a lot of my life happens," she jokes.

They blew into January's Canadian championships with mounting confidence. The Nationals were held at London's beautiful John Labatt Centre, just twenty minutes south of Ilderton, and because of the adoring hometown crowd's energy and their heavy-favourite status they treated it like a "mini-Olympics." Although "they knew every volunteer" and had some connection to nearly half the crowd, they remained in their bubble, kept mostly to themselves, and concentrated on presenting three consecutive good skates for the first time that season.

"I was starting to believe that if we had a good OD one day we wouldn't have a good free

---

"OFF THE ICE, OUR RELATIONSHIP WAS BETTER THAN IT'S EVER BEEN AND I CAME AWAY FROM THE NATIONALS FEELING THAT WE WERE GOING TO WIN THE OLYMPICS. BUT THREE DAYS LATER, WHEN I WAS CRYING AT THE RINK AND COULDN'T SKATE BECAUSE MY LEGS WERE IN PAIN, I WAS FEELING LIKE WE DIDN'T EVEN DESERVE TO BE ON THE TEAM." — *Tessa*

---

from The Goose and make changes to their flamenco Original Dance. "We connected," Tessa smiles. "We were talking but there was more that we weren't saying that was understood. It was the first time that we had felt that again."

BACK IN CANTON, TESSA AND SCOTT WENT into high gear, training more intensely than they'd been able to for the better part of two years. They worked again with Luis Montero and really grew into their flamenco characters, changed some of the side-by-side footwork with Marina and Igor's permission, elevated their speed and power, and became much more explosive in their OD presentation. Tessa was still experiencing pain in her legs, but had learned how to train around it. One day before Christmas, she was able to make it through her first double run-through of the free dance in two seasons, and she and Scott celebrated at the nearby Bob Evans Restaurant,

dance the next," Scott says. "But I knew I had to challenge myself to do three in a row."

They skated brilliantly in all three segments, with their OD showing particular improvement after all the hard work, and won their third Canadian title. After their flamenco, Marina called them into the women's dressing room ("THAT was awkward," Scott quips) and said, 'I'm telling you the story now because you performed that program so well; but of the hundreds and hundreds of flamencos that you listened to and found only ONE that you liked, it was the one song that [her legendary pair] Gordeeva and Grinkov also chose for their flamenco.'"

"Off the ice, our relationship was better than it's ever been," Tessa says, "and I came away from the Nationals feeling that we were going to win the Olympics. But three days later, when I was crying at the rink and couldn't skate because my legs were in pain, I was feeling like we didn't even deserve to be on the team."

Above: Tessa and Scott receive a warm send-off at John Labatt Centre a month prior to the 2010 Games.

But through more than a year of setbacks they had learned how to recover emotionally and physically and build their training back up slowly. They fit in one week of run-throughs, and worked on the Olympic compulsory, the Tango Romantica, with Elena Tchaikovskaya, who had helped her hall of fame students, Alexander Gorshkov and Lyudmila Pakhomova, invent the dance in the mid-1970s.

MEANWHILE OLYMPIC FEVER, FUELLED BY A cross-continent torch relay, was seizing Canada. One benefit of being in the U.S. and having to focus so much on Tessa's shins, training alternatives, and making it through one competition at a time was that they had too much to worry about and were never overcome by Olympic jitters. "We knew that as long as we did as much as we could that we would be happy," Scott says. "And that became the goal. I mean, you wake up every day, and you go to sleep every night, praying and dreaming about the Olympics. There's no doubt about that. But there were never any negative feelings about the Olympics."

Tessa and Scott were helped greatly in their positive approach to the pressure-packed Games by the experience of 2002 Olympic pairs champion David Pelletier, who had joined their team as an advisor, and eventually began acting in an agent capacity for the young Canadians.

Above: Waiting for their flight to Vancouver, B.C., February 11, 2010.
Right: Tessa and Scott at the Vancouver 2010 Winter Olympics Opening Ceremonies.

Right: The Opening Ceremonies of The 2010 Vancouver Olympics.
Below: With Igor, Marina, and Elena Tchaikovskaya, who helped choreograph their Tango Romantica compulsory program.

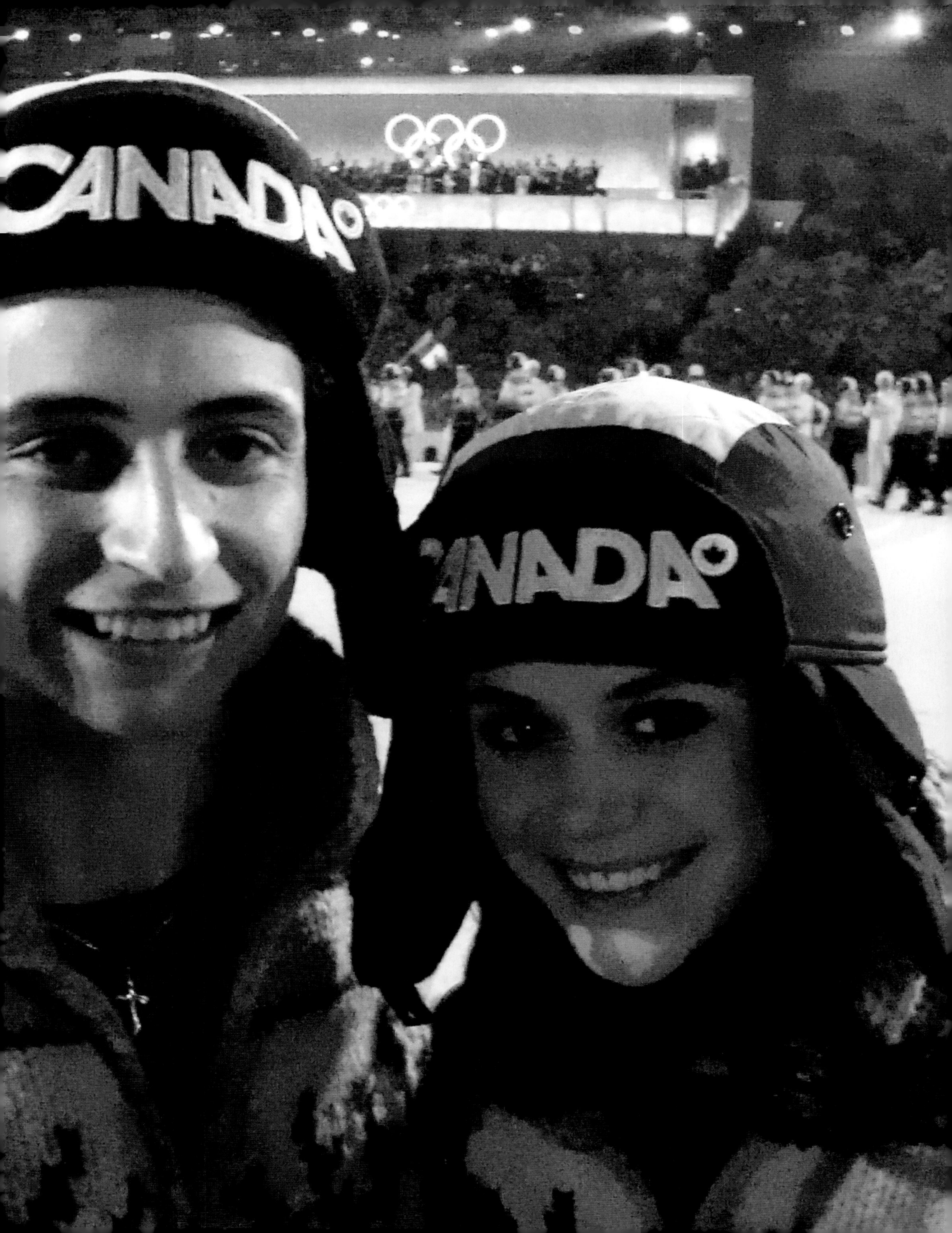
CANADA
CANADA

"He was a critical member of our support team," Tessa says. "A wonderful mentor and a 'go-to' person for us leading into the Games. He'd been there before and knew what to expect."

And on February 11, Tessa, Scott, and Marina flew to Vancouver.

"I was in shock in the athletes' village for the first two or three days," Tessa says. "It was overwhelming, there was so much to take in, and there are so many athletes. You're kind of unsure if you belong."

"You wanted to be up in the lounge with people, and then you wanted to be watching the athletes," Scott said. "I'm glad we went a week early for our first one because you really have to learn in the village to not get consumed with everything. It's amazing, it's the best feeling in the world to be there with the team."

Skate Canada had booked extra ice time over four days in nearby Port Moody — and Tessa and Scott had arranged for Meryl and Charlie to work out there, too — but things took a turn for the worse. One day her shin pain was so bad that Tessa was having trouble breathing. Again, they took it easy, and by the time they had their first official practice at the Pacific Coliseum, on the first day of the Games, they were back in top form. There was no one in the stands, but "the energy in the building was perfect," Tessa recalls.

They arrived at the Opening Ceremonies at BC Place and were surprised that they had to line up "for hours and hours" awaiting the athletes' parade. They both say that had they had to compete the next day they could not have taken part, but it was all worth it as they entered the stadium, with Marina beside them, proud to be representing the country that had first taken her in.

"We were in the tunnel [waiting to walk into the arena] and heard 'Canada' and the roar that went with it," Scott recalls, dropping his jaw in awe.

Opposite: With Marina in Vancouver. *Above:* Athletes' parade at BC Place.
Right: In the athletes' village.

"We were in shock. I said to Tessa in the line, 'I'm nervous because it's our country that's on display. If they don't do a great job, I'm going to feel kind of responsible.' But all the athletes kept saying all week, 'Best Games Ever, Best Games Ever.' We felt so proud to be Canadian and be a part of these Games."

"It was amazing when we first heard 'Canada' after our names back when we started skating internationally," Tessa says. "But this just felt as if we were part of something much bigger. And everyone was coming together for this. That was unbelievable. UN-believable."

It was to be one of the most memorable Winter Games ever — partly for the wrong reasons. Earlier that morning, Georgian luger Nodar Kumaritashvili had been killed in a horrific training accident at Whistler. The de facto spokesman for the Georgian athletes became Otar Japaridze, an ice dancer whom the Canadians knew.

"[Nodar] went to the Games, just like we did. They're supposed to be *games*," Tessa says.

But all elite athletes are trained to shut out even the worst circumstances, and Tessa and Scott had three competition segments to prepare for. "We were back on track off the ice, in terms of our relationship, so marching through that together was such a team thing for us, it was just like this," Tessa says, clasping her hands tightly. "We did everything together for the entire Olympics."

They had some excellent practices, but two days before the compulsories, Tessa's shins acted up and prevented them from doing a full runthrough in a free dance practice attended by many judges. They became nervous.

"We knew we had to make a good first impression," Scott explains. "Tessa was talking to me and I wasn't even listening. I was zoned out — she actually had to grab my hand. And say 'Hey, hey, we're here, it's us.' And somehow, I don't know

how, I snapped out of it when we got back on the ice. I was still extremely nervous. But we skated well. Marina was so happy. She said, 'You need to skate like that. Who cares about the Olympics? That was amazing.'"

It may be that any rogue nerves, which would have undermined them in competition, were flushed out that day. When the ice dancing competition opened with compulsories on Friday, February 19, Tessa and Scott hugged each other during the warm-up in a way that soon became part of their ritual. "We feel each other breathing, just to make sure that we're together," she says. Practising breathing correctly was important in Tessa's physiotherapy because it helped get oxygen to her shins more efficiently. The crowd had gone completely crazy when they were announced during warm-up, and Tessa and Scott allowed themselves to absorb that positive energy before returning to their "just-you-and-I" bubble. Halfway through their Tango Romantica, it was obvious to even the untrained eye that they were skating magnificently, and the audience began clapping so loudly that Scott kept yelling at Tessa to keep focused.

"We've never been more in tune with each other," Tessa grins. "Never been more together. It was the *best!*"

"We were ecstatic. Until we got the marks," Scott said.

"I was still happy," Tessa says. "Scott wasn't."

Scott, angry that they had finished second, was miming to the judges: "Just wait until Sunday," when the Original Dance would be held. But Tessa thought, "'We're second. We're going to win the Olympics.' I knew it. My older brother Casey was flying in that night and I told him on the phone, 'Don't worry, Case, we're going to wait to get the gold after you arrive.'"

There was a practice day Saturday, with another early-morning practice on Sunday, the day of the Original Dance. Tessa was rooming at the village with Joannie Rochette, one of the medal contenders in women's singles. At around

"WE'VE NEVER BEEN MORE IN TUNE WITH EACH OTHER. NEVER BEEN MORE TOGETHER. IT WAS THE *BEST!*" —*Tessa*

"WE WERE ECSTATIC. UNTIL WE GOT THE MARKS." —*Scott*

Left: First day of Olympic competition, skating compulsory dance Tango Romantica.

5:30 a.m. Sunday, while Tessa was in the washroom quietly preparing for practice, she heard a noise and thought she had woken her roommate. "Then there was a knock on the bathroom door and I walked out and I saw everyone from Skate Canada in the common room and in our room," Tessa recalls. "I was wondering what was going on when Jo walked by me to go into the washroom and said, calmly, 'My mom died.' Just like that. Benoît Lavoie [Skate Canada president] told me what happened."

Thérèse Rochette, just fifty-five, had arrived in Vancouver with her husband Normand only the day before, and had collapsed and died late Saturday night. Normand and Skate Canada officials decided to let Joannie get some sleep before telling her the unspeakable news.

"They told me to keep my usual routine, which meant doing my hair and makeup for practice," Tessa says. "So I went into the washroom with her and we were doing our makeup side-by-side. Finally I stopped and gave her her space and went to a different washroom. I just said, 'I'm so sorry,' and 'Your mom's with you.'" I was in shock. It didn't really register."

Both Tessa and Scott felt selfish that they had to practise and concentrate on their own medal pursuit when a close friend had endured such a tragedy. But it's the ability to temporarily prevent anything from distracting them from their goals that sets elite athletes apart. Joannie Rochette herself is the same way. Before leaving for practice, though, Scott automatically wondered if his own parents would be in the stands, and that's when it hit him and he broke down crying. "Jo would never get to have that. Her mom would never see her at the Games." Tessa's voice cracks when she recalls that Kate Virtue was in the stands that morning. Tessa and Scott continually squeezed each other's hand for support, and on the bus home Tessa broke down and so they talked about the situation rather than ignore it. Scott reminded Tessa that the media would want her to comment about Joannie after the OD, and Tessa said she could handle it.

Their realization of what had happened grew over the day, but as they came to the rink for the Original Dance, Tessa and Scott were ready, telling each other that their hearts were with Joannie but they had a job to do.

"And then we went out and skated our asses off," Scott says.

With Tessa flipping her gorgeous red skirt to the beat of the music and Scott in perfect Spanish character it was a sultry, sizzling, technically demanding performance — and when they finished they both yelled, "Yes!" The crowd erupted, and then erupted again when the Canadians moved into first place. At home in Ontario, Paul MacIntosh was thinking that he had just seen the greatest Original Dance ever performed in competition.

IT WAS AN IMPORTANT NIGHT NOT JUST TO THE skaters but the overall Canadian Olympic team. The men's hockey team had been beaten that night by the U.S. and spirits were down, especially since it had become clear that Canada was not going to win the medal count as the country's Olympic program "Own the Podium" had all but promised. Yet Scott knew the second week was going to be Canada's strong point, and it was slowly emerging the country was going to win more gold medals than ever before. As it turned out, they won more gold medals than any other country *ever* had.

And for the first time in two years, Tessa and Scott were glad they didn't have a day off after a competition. They wanted to keep the momentum alive. Moreover, Tessa's legs were fine because she had had time between morning practice and evening competition to undergo physiotherapy.

After morning practice on February 22, Tessa and Scott each battled their own demons. Both were engaged in positive thinking, trying to replay a successful program in their minds. But Scott kept imagining a three-turn in which Tessa's skate sliced him. Tessa was having a similar experience during physio as she played the Mahler piece over and over again on her iPod. After twenty minutes, Mary Brannagan asked her why a four-minute program was taking so long to listen to. "I can't get past this part where we mess up," she said. "It took

Opposite: Original Dance skated to "Farrucas" by Pepe Romero.

me all day to get through the four-minute program. But then I did it several times."

"If you ever want to get to know yourself," Scott says, "try those last twelve hours before an Olympic final. You have so much time with your own thoughts, absolutely everything that could happen goes through your mind."

Tessa and Scott were scheduled to skate third from the end, and as they stroked out to take their opening positions, Tessa said, "This is our time, we deserve this." A packed arena, and several million Canadian television fans, agreed.

"We're here, kiddo," Scott said.

"Showtime!" Tessa said in her standard response.

From the first note they were in absolute sync, capturing the haunting rises and falls of the Mahler symphony so exactly that at first the crowd was dead silent in awe. Then, as it became apparent that they were witnessing history, the spectators grew as loud as the music while Tessa and Scott, exquisite in their execution and timing, stayed completely in the "zone."

"Watching that was probably one of the most

Below: Free dance skated to Mahler's "Symphony no. 5." *Opposite:* "The Goose" during the Olympic free dance program.

magical moments of my life," Igor says. "I felt secure. I was surprised I wasn't nervous, but I knew they were going to do it. I'd seen them do it a million times in practice at home. At the same time, though, I did every step with them."

Marina said that when she watched Scott and Tessa skate, she was transported away from the usual technical worries of a coach. "I was just melting," she said.

"Until the last five seconds we were perfect," Scott says, explaining that in the final, dizzying, spinning lift, with the spectators on their feet screaming and hundreds of them crying, they had come out, over Tessa's objection, facing away from the judges, not toward them.

"Thirteen years together and I have learned this lesson," Scott laughs. "When you think you're

Left: Tessa and Scott performing their free dance at the 2010 Olympic Games. *Right:* On the podium during the medal ceremony.

right and Tessa thinks she's right, chances are Tessa's right. We were just looking at each other: 'Seriously, we have three great programs and the last five seconds we screwed it up?' But Marina said, 'Not a chance. That was great.'"

The judges agreed, awarding them 110.42 points, the highest of their career, and four tens in the program components. Their combined score was 221.57, nearly six points higher than Meryl Davis and Charlie White. Everyone knew they were looking at the new Olympic ice dancing champions, the youngest ever and the first from North America.

"Scott kept saying to me, 'Look at this, take this in,'" Tessa says of the pandemonium in the arena.

"We were so happy," Scott says. "You *are* thinking about the journey, how everything came together. About how much your families have helped you. About everything we've gone through, and how it was all worth it. Every second of it."

BACK IN ILDERTON, AT A GATHERING ORGANIZED by Carol and Paul Moir, 300 people were crammed into the Community Centre watching the free skate on three large TVs.

"My older sister Marg and I were grasping hands during the free dance, and when the marks went up, we jumped and screamed and hugged the grandpas," Carol Moir says. "It was one big hugfest, 300 of us hugging. Then we had to wait for the other two free dances. It was the longest wait. And then we did it all again."

In Waterloo, Paul MacIntosh and his wife Carolyn Allwright "were jumping around our living room like mad people." Paul had eaten a club sandwich earlier, because when he was coaching Tessa and Scott he'd had one for lunch at a novice event and they had performed well, so he kept doing it for their biggest competitions, long after they'd moved to Canton. And his lucky "Be the class of the ice" e-mails were among the handful that Tessa hadn't had blocked out during Olympic week.

In the Pacific Coliseum, Suzanne Killing-Wood, whose sixteen-month-old daughter Gracie had learned to say "Tessa" shortly before Suzanne left home "to watch Tessa and Scott win," had been amazed at the awe the audience expressed while watching her former students skate.

Left: Marina, Scott, Tessa, and Igor celebrate after hearing their scores for the free dance.

"I started crying after three seconds. I was so proud. I just kept thinking how happy they were going to feel when they finished. When they knew they had done everything they possibly could, at the right moment, in their home country in front of their friends and family."

Jordan Virtue was also crying over the long journey it had been. She was sitting with her mother in the first row on the judges' side, with the rest of the family sitting in twos around the rink.

"I was nervous after I saw Meryl and Charlie's marks," Kate Virtue recalls. "They were

ing, 'Thank you, guys, thank you so much. Thanks for the medals, and for being part of this with us. This is the coolest feeling.' When it actually felt real was *on* the podium when we got the medals."

As Tessa and Scott "kept bouncing around" waiting for the medal ceremony, Marina was explaining to reporters how Canadian she felt, and how she felt the same way about the Mahler program that she had about creating ethereal routines for Gordeeva and Grinkov.

"You will never design a program like this without love," Marina told the *Hamilton Spectator*.

"'O CANADA' STARTED TO PLAY AND EVERYONE STARTED TO SING. IT WAS CRAZY. I COULD FEEL SCOTT'S ENERGY AND WE JUST KEPT LOOKING AT EACH OTHER. WE BOTH SANG: THERE WAS NO MICROPHONE LUCKILY. THAT WAS THE MOST FUN I EVER HAD." — *Tessa*

---

so high and they skated better than they had all year. But when Tessa and Scott took their positions on the ice, they looked so calm and controlled I relaxed. And I wanted to savour every moment."

Alma Moir was also calm when she saw that her son and Tessa were at ease when they reached centre ice. She and Joe Moir, Danny and his girl-friend, Charlie and his wife, first cousin Cara Moir, and good friends Ron and Lynn Lee had abandoned their scattered seats for an obscured-vision spot above the kiss and cry so they could all be together.

"When I saw the marks go up, there was no time to react because Joe and I had to go down to see the kids downstairs," Alma says. "When I saw them I thought, 'Did you really just win the Olympics?'"

In the kiss and cry, Tessa said to Igor, "Oh my God, I think we're Olympic champions," and he replied that he thought she was right, although Scott didn't want to jinx it until after the final two had skated. "We were so happy," Scott says. "I just wanted to thank the audience. I remember think-

"A general love, I mean. A love for a country, and a love for music. And a love for a man and a woman doing beautiful skating."

As they headed for the podium, Tessa thought "about the number of people who have helped us in thirteen years: the people who have given up so much time and money and energy. It wasn't just us. Yes, we were the two out there who were skating, but there was so much behind us. When we were on the medal stand Scott said, 'Look, no one left the rink.' There were thousands of people there, and usually at medals there are ten people, including our parents. We had so many moments that we just looked at each other and said, 'This is it! This is what we've been dreaming of.' We'd already talked a little bit about just having fun and forgetting to stand properly, forget that the cameras would be on us. I think I said, 'Can I hold your hand?' Then 'O Canada' started to play and everyone started to sing. It was crazy. I could feel Scott's energy and we just kept looking at each other. We both sang: there was no microphone luckily. That was the most fun I've ever had."

Opposite: Tessa and Scott celebrate on the podium after winning the gold medal in ice dance.

*Opposite:
(clockwise from top)* Approaching the stands after the medal ceremony; Tessa smiling after the medal ceremony; Scott hugging his brothers Danny and Charlie in the stands.
Left: On the podium after the presentation of the medals.

vancouver 2010

2010

After media interviews, Tessa had her name drawn for doping control. The forty-five minutes of testing took her away from Scott and her family, causing her an eerie feeling of separation in the greatest hour of her young life. To fill the time Scott went out to the empty arena. "I just snuck out there and I kissed the rings, and suddenly the five people still in there broke out cheering." They were maintenance staff, and Scott climbed into the stands to have his picture taken with them.

After a celebration with their families at a downtown restaurant, they did interviews until 8 a.m., had ninety minutes of sleep — Scott couldn't nod off, so called all his buddies and his uncle — then spent most of the next day doing more media interviews. They spent the rest of the time together, enjoying the Olympics, cheering for the hockey teams, and attending Joannie

Opposite: Celebrating on the podium.
Above: On the ice with the Canadian flag.
Below: Scott in the empty arena after the gold medal win.

Clockwise from top: Media interviews;
(left to right) Joe, Alma, Scott, Danny, and
Charlie Moir celebrating at a downtown
restaurant; Tessa celebrating with brother
Casey; with medals at a press conference.
Opposite: Tessa and Scott attend
men's hockey events during the Games.

Top: Posing with coaches Igor and Marina and fellow skaters Charlie White and Meryl Davis during the Games.
Bottom: Tessa and Scott are greeted on the tarmac by Alma and Joe Moir and Kate Virtue after arriving home from the Games, March 2010.
Opposite: Tessa and Scott entering London Airport.

Rochette's inspiring bronze medal triumph over her unfathomable grief. They celebrated with the rest of the country when Sidney Crosby's overtime goal, the last moment of the actual Games, gave Canada its record fourteenth gold medal.

Not once in that afterglow did they even consider skipping the following month's world championships in Turin. They had decided in January that they wanted to win the Olympics, then the Worlds, because they'd never had that title. But each would eventually discover why the last three Olympic ice dance champions had not attended the ensuing Worlds. Back in Canton, Tessa found that her body was tired from two years of injury and worry, and because she hadn't had time for as much physiotherapy her shins were "awful." After all the Olympic adrenalin it was hard to get motivated for those seven-hour days at the training rink. Scott, meanwhile, was excited during training, but when they got to Turin their viewpoints flipped. He found that while he had his usual competition nerves, he was without his competitive edge, while Tessa was in full competition mode.

However, they skated well in the Golden Waltz compulsory, and then set a world record with 70.27 points in the Original Dance. That was despite being informed before the warm-up, through Skate Canada and Marina, that the judging panel was likely going to declare their final lift illegal, which would cost them two points. "We decided not to think about it until we got there and just winged it," Tessa says, "and I don't even remember what we did." But they avoided the deduction that would have cost them the world title. Scott had trouble with a twizzle during the free dance, and Meryl and Charlie won the segment to finish second. "But technically it was good, we weren't cautious, and I think it was really a good way to end the season," Scott says.

Right: On the ice during the exhibition gala at the World Championships in Turin, Italy, March 2010.

So, while there had never been an Olympic ice dance champion from North America and no world champion before 2003, Canadians had now won both the Worlds and Olympics in the same season with Americans right behind them in both. The power base had clearly shifted, although Tessa and Scott weren't dwelling on that.

"Ice dancing should be a North American force," Scott says flatly.

"It comes back to being the eight- and ten-year-olds that were always the smallest and youngest team," Tessa adds. "We were always battling with that, so battling as North Americans was just part of the story. No one told us we couldn't do it."

"ICE DANCING SHOULD BE A NORTH AMERICAN FORCE"—*Scott*

Left: Final moments of the free dance program at the Worlds, 2010.
Opposite: On the podium at the Worlds.

Tessa and Scott are struck by the contrast between the photos on their podium at Worlds and those from the Olympics. In Vancouver, they were joyous and full of abandon while in Turin they were visibly tired. It had been a long, emotionally exhausting battle back from injury and off-ice estrangement. But they had captured hearts across Canada, had elevated ice dancing far beyond what it had ever been in the country, and had proven that they were correct when they left Ilderton to pursue their Olympic dream.

"When they finished their Olympic free dance after having been through so much, I was thinking that there were these eight- and ten-year-olds who set a goal, and they achieved it," Kate Virtue marvels. "Who does that in life?"

Tessa and Scott had done it. And it was time to take their ultimate achievement back to its roots.

"There are
so many people
who want
to meet you,
and you have
the ability to
affect them,
to see their smiles.
In that way
it has changed
a lot for us." —*Scott*

Chapter Six

THE FUTURE

HAVING REALIZED THEIR CHILDHOOD DREAM, TESSA AND SCOTT TURN THEIR ATTENTION TO THE FUTURE.

AS FAR BACK AS HE CAN REMEMBER, SCOTT has always loved the Ilderton Fair Parade. It signals the start of the Ilderton Fair, one of the oldest and most honoured agricultural fairs in Ontario, kicking off an early autumn weekend of excitement and community celebration, virtually in his own backyard. Every year he'd thrill to the floats and marchers as they proceeded slowly from the post office down Ilderton Road and into the fair-grounds. And eventually he

got to be part of the procession. In recognition of their skating achievements, he and Tessa have appeared in the parade a half-dozen times.

"We always used to joke that Scott thought the Ilderton Fair was a national holiday," Tessa laughs.

"I still do," Scott laughs back.

Because the parade conflicted with intense training for the Grand Prix circuit, Scott hadn't made it home for fair weekend for two or three years, but on June 12, 2010, he and Tessa were honoured with their own procession through town. And it meant more to both of them than even the hallowed Ilderton Fair Parade.

Opposite: A photo of Tessa and Scott that appeared in *International Figure Skating* magazine.
Above: Fans at London Airport.
Right: Two young fans with painted faces wait to greet Tessa and Scott.

ILDERTON
LIONS

ARENA
AND
CURLING CLUB

SCOTT & TESSA
ARE COMING
JUNE 12
PARADE 3PM

13168

As Tessa and Scott rode in a horse and buggy, following torch bearers and their families — also carried in a horse and buggy — toward the arena, the streets were lined several-deep with cheering well-wishers, most of them clad in bright nationalistic red. The Canadian flag was everywhere, kids wore shirts bearing the Olympic slogan "Believe!" and one lawn even displayed a three-foot-tall wooden cutout of a Canada goose with a sign "The Goose Is Golden," in honour of their suddenly legendary creative lift. Reflecting the

That's where it started for Scott and I — in that rink. Everyone has watched us grow up, and we felt that support. We felt that from the very beginning when we were heading off to sectional championships, not just for the Olympics."

And something extraordinary happened to a number of the celebrants, something they could never have predicted, because they had assumed that February 22 would always stand without equal. Yet some eighty days later, Tessa found that the feelings of pride, thankfulness, and excitement

> "PHENOMENAL. IT WAS A PRETTY EMOTIONAL DAY. WE DIDN'T THINK THERE'D BE SO MANY PEOPLE TO COME OUT AND SUPPORT US." —*Scott*

casual but deeply appreciative nature of the celebrations, when the entourage reached For Pizza's Sake, the restaurant where Charlie Moir once worked, a pizza was delivered to their buggy.

"Phenomenal," Scott says, searching for the right description. "It was a pretty emotional day. We didn't think there'd be so many people to come out and support us."

With 3,000 friends and fans crammed inside the arena for ceremonies and another 1,000 overflow tickets sold for the adjacent curling rink, the turnout was at least double the population of Ilderton.

"The support they showed was unbelievable," Tessa marvels. "And what was so cool was that everyone had been there from the beginning.

overcame her again, in exactly the same way, with exactly the same force.

"We thought we'd never feel that way again, but we all relived it on that weekend too," said their first coach, Carol Moir. Her twin sister, Alma, Scott's mother, echoed that surprise, turning to Kate Virtue and whispering, as a video of the gold medal free dance was shown on the giant arena screens, "I can't believe how nervous I am, and I know how it all turns out."

Tessa was impressed by a replay of the video of the Ilderton Community Centre on February 22, packed to the rafters "and everyone going crazy. Part of me kind of wishes I was there that night. It was cool to see all that energy and the community pride."

Opposite: (top) Tessa and Scott wave to fans as they move along the parade route. *(Bottom)* A float arriving at the Ilderton Arena. *Above: (left)* The crowd outside the Ilderton Arena. *(Right)* Members of the Virtue and Moir families ride along the parade route.

Top: On the ice during a Roots photoshoot. *Bottom:* On the ice in Korea with skaters.

SINCE THE WORLDS, TESSA AND SCOTT HAVE toured the country with "Stars on Ice," signed a promotional contract with internationally renowned Canadian clothing retailer Roots (who will give Tessa a chance to try her hand at fashion design, starting with purses), been honoured at NHL games, done shows in South Korea, made numerous other public appearances, and have been instantly recognized everywhere.

"One thing that has been really great since the Olympics is that I'm amazed at just how polite and courteous and respectful everyone is," Tessa says. "If someone comes up to us in the middle of dinner, in airports, or on the street, they just wish us well. Everyone is so nice, so sweet, so polite, and so Canadian."

The Olympic champions feel that, at their core, they are the same people who left home at thirteen and fifteen to conquer the figure skating

Above: Dropping the puck at an NHL game with fellow Olympic gold medallist Jennifer Botterill, March 2010.

world, but Scott says that the Ilderton reception, and the manner in which they're received everywhere in Canada, have been eye-openers.

"There are so many people who want to meet you, and you have the ability to affect them, to see their smiles, to see the reaction of so many children," says Scott, who had quietly taken his gold medal back to Oxbow Public School on a brief stopover after the Games. "So you want to try to influence the children to dream big and reach

for the stars, which is so powerful. In that way, it has changed a lot for us. And there are responsibilities that come with being Olympic champions that Tess and I have every intention of fulfilling. As people, we really feel like we're just Tessa and Scott. I feel I'm still the same Scott going back to Ilderton every weekend, and next time I go I'm pretty sure there won't be a parade. We still feel like we didn't know why everybody was there that day. It feels like we're just us, but I guess we have some more

responsibilities to take care of than we did before."

One of those responsibilities is dealing with the constant public scrutiny, realizing that every set of eyes in every room, on every street corner they pass, is always on them. And there is the constant probing from the media about their relationship — best friends, business partners, lifelong soul mates, but not a romantic couple — and about their skating future. Tessa and Scott really didn't know until a few weeks after the 2010 world championships if they would compete in the 2010–11 season. And once they decided to make a commitment to the 2011 Worlds, they still didn't know if they'd be around for 2012, let alone the 2014 Olympic Games in Sochi, Russia.

Left: Tessa and Scott speaking in front of fans.
Below: (top) Meeting Prince Albert of Monaco.
(Bottom) At a parade during the Calgary Stampede.

"After 2011 Worlds, we'll have to re-evaluate again," Tessa explains. "We can't think about four years right now, we have to think about it one year at a time. In the years heading to Vancouver we knew that 2010 was the commitment. But we have to narrow our focus and not get too overwhelmed with the idea of training for four more years. The 2014 Olympics could likely happen for us, but we just don't know."

One attraction to the eligible ranks is that in June 2010 the ISU, as expected, dropped the compulsory dances from senior events. That reduces ice dancing competition to the newly-named Short Dance and the free dance — bringing it in line with the other three disciplines, which have had only two segments since single compulsory figures

> "AFTER 2011 WORLDS, WE'LL HAVE TO RE-EVALUATE AGAIN. WE CAN'T THINK ABOUT FOUR YEARS RIGHT NOW, WE HAVE TO THINK ABOUT IT ONE YEAR AT A TIME." — *Tessa*

were abandoned in 1990. Most elite ice dancers, including Tessa and Scott, applaud the move because compulsories took up between sixty to ninety minutes of ice time per day during peak training periods. In their absence, "you can spend more time artistically," Tessa says.

And that's important to the young Canadians, who take their role as the world's top-ranked ice dancers seriously and want to help steer their discipline in a healthy direction. When they refer to artistry, they don't talk about it as separate from the technical and athletic components of skating. They see them as integrated, one blending into the other seamlessly. Their Olympic-season free dance program demonstrated that kind of flowing harmony, but they feel it can be stretched even farther. And, having won both Olympics and Worlds, they feel they now can put slightly more

Right: Tessa and Scott pose for photographer Myra Klarman.

Above and Opposite: A training session at the Arctic Edge rink in Canton, Michigan.

emphasis on creativity than on pursuing victory, although winning is still the ultimate goal, especially to a pair as ultra-competitive as they are.

"Something that Tess and I are passionate about is true dancing on the ice," Scott says. "Moving well on the ice and not being over-theatrical, or having those programs we've been used to seeing in ice dancing over the last ten years; those kind of in-your-face programs. We want to go back to movement, which is more dance-y, and makes people feel good and have fun. We have two really big titles under our belt and we have the opportunity, with the new rules coming in, to push the sport, and if we're the people able to do that, great."

One complication is that even though com-pulsory dances have been dropped, some of the rules and requirements have actually been tight-ened, especially in the new Short Dance. While that is meant to help keep the "sport" component from being overshadowed by the "art" component, it does put restrictions on how far even the most creative teams can push the artistic envelope.

"We want to go in a different direction, try new things, and push the bound-aries," Tessa says. "But there's only so much you can do, especially with the rules, and unfortunately we're learning there could be even more restrictions. It's a balance. We do want to move the sport and

"WE WANT TO
GO IN A DIFFERENT
DIRECTION,
TRY NEW THINGS,
AND PUSH THE
BOUNDARIES." —*Tessa*

challenge ourselves, but we also still want to win, so we have to satisfy the judges and satisfy the ISU committee. We have to please so many people. I think that's where you struggle: there are only so many ways you can do your footwork to get a Level 4, and unfortunately, to get that Level 4, you can't really do anything 'out there.' I think that is our challenge with the lifts too: we want the lifts to make sense. It has to be a complete package; we don't want to break up a complete storyline just to do a lift which will get us a Level 4. Part of our job is to figure out that balance."

Creating balance is a major focus in their lives, both on and off the ice. Weathering the tests of competing at the highest level, living away from home, being together from a younger age and for a longer time than most dance couples, and coping with the fear and anxiety induced by Tessa's injury, Tessa and Scott have learned a great deal about each other and about themselves as a partnership. Their history is unique among championship dancers, with the closest parallel being, perhaps fittingly, Meryl Davis and Charlie White. Tessa and Scott grew up only a fifteen-minute drive from each other, yet never had to look farther afield for a partner or best friend. Their Olympic aspirations, unspoken as they might have been, started while their non-skating peers were still playing hopscotch. They got together at such a young age that not only Tessa and Scott, but their parents and coaches too, have always quickly replied "seven and nine" when asked about how old they were when they were paired up. It was only after the Olympics that they redid the math and were surprised to find that they were actually eight and ten years old when Carol Moir asked the young gymnast from London to compare heights with her nephew. That confusion is a result of them growing into their partnership organically, rather than having a defined, structured beginning. In effect they can't really remember *not* being together.

Aside from the most glaring statistic — that they are the youngest ice dancers ever to win the Olympic gold medal — there are other strong

Right: Tessa and Scott during a photoshoot with photographer Myra Klarman.

indicators of just how rare their combination of youth, longevity, and competitive success actually is. For instance, in the forty-five years that Canada has held senior, junior, and novice national ice dancing championships, only two couples have won all three titles: Louise Lind and Barry Soper, who eventually married each other, and the brother-and-sister team of Karyn and Rod Garossino. Had Tessa and Scott been allowed to remain in novice for a second year, they likely would have been the third dance team to make the novice-junior-senior sweep, and the first who were neither siblings nor romantically involved. Further, the world junior figure skating

we've been trying to figure out how to make up new moves and be very original," Tessa says. "So we need what we both bring to the team. I know we've been together for thirteen years, but we want to come up with things that have never been done before, so we're still learning more about each other and how we work together. It's an ongoing process."

They also recognize that a strong competitive environment raises the bar for everybody, and they're very encouraged about the state of ice dancing in North America. A strong history of "pure skating," as Scott calls it, combined with embracing the new scoring system and the influx

"CANADIANS HAVE A DIFFERENT WAY OF SKATING, THEY HAVE A DIFFERENT WAY OF PUSHING AND GLIDING. YOU CAN SEE IT IN THE YOUNGER SKATERS COMING UP. WE'RE DOING SOMETHING RIGHT." —*Tessa*

championships have been held annually since 1976, and in the more than three decades since, only two ice dancing teams have won the world junior championship and gone on, partnership intact, to win the world senior championship. Others have won junior with one partner and senior with another but only Russian ice dancers Oksana Domnina and Maxim Shabalin (2003 and 2009) and Tessa and Scott (2006 and 2010) have pulled off double Worlds victories. And only Tessa and Scott have won both the world junior championship and an Olympic gold medal. That is partly due to the Code of Points, which judges performance rather than reputation, undermining the old "wait-your-turn" process, which ruled ice dancing for more than half a century. But it is due mostly to Tessa and Scott's firm commitment to and love for each other, the strength of the relationship between their two sets of parents, the fact that they did most of their growing up side by side, the healthy competition between the best friends making up the dance team, and the hard-won ability to recognize and embrace how they are the same, how they differ, and how their similarities and differences play important roles in the creative process.

"Especially over the last couple of years,

of Russian coaches, with their deep background in dance, has shifted the balance of ice dance across the Atlantic Ocean from Europe. Tessa and Scott are particularly impressed by ice dancing's status, and depth, in Canada.

"We heard from Alexei Yagudin that he never watched ice dancing before but now, with the new system, he does watch it. As a sport we're going to thrive off of that, which you can already see if you go to a novice or a junior championship. There are some sensational ice dance teams in Canada. Very young and very talented. We were in Korea doing a couple of shows and a lot of the skaters were saying, 'Canadians have a different way of skating, they have a different way of pushing and gliding,'" Tessa adds, praising the CanSkate instructional program on which both she and Scott were reared. "You can see it in the younger skaters coming up. We're doing something right; there are kids coming up who have that talent, that charisma, and that drive. There aren't any limits for those young Canadian skaters, and not just in dance. It's great: we want to be challenged and pushed."

They both say there should no longer be any debate about whether figure skating is a sport or a performance art. Tessa emphasizes that with the

Above: Tessa on set for a television interview.
Right: Scott with hockey teammates.

Code of Points there are "clear guidelines, so you can compare teams directly. It is a sport, for sure." And while the artistry makes the average fan see only the calm surface of the duck, the judges are now seeing, and marking the furious paddling that goes on below.

That furious paddling involves sacrifices that are both obvious and subtle. Tessa and Scott have always been aware that their families have made great sacrifices for them on several fronts — time, financing, and forgoing family vacations, among others — and are thankful for it. And they are also grateful that their families never let them feel that anything could ever get in the way of, as Tessa describes it, "something I was going after from a young age."

Naturally the skaters themselves were making great sacrifices too. The primary one, they agree, was the normal teenage school experience. Scott calls getting his high school diploma "priority one," and Tessa has always felt the strong pull of the classroom and the life that surrounds it. Her mother recalls that when Tessa finally did enroll at Windsor's Holy Names for grade eleven (after completing online courses for a term while in Canton), she bubbled with the small details of the school day. "I'd be driving her to school in Windsor and she'd say, 'Mom there are students sitting beside me!'" Kate Virtue recalls. "Or 'You can just put up your hand and the teacher will ask you a question,' and 'You know that smell that's always at a high school? I even like that.' She was so excited and happy. And one of the things she's most proud of was that she was able to graduate from high school at the same time that the kids she started kindergarten with did."

Elite skaters also sacrifice the ebb and flow of social relationships that would normally occur in their teens and early twenties. Tessa and Scott spend hours and hours together but they don't date each other, and as long as skating dominates their lives there isn't a lot of time for others.

"We spend so much time and energy focusing on that one goal, I think someone who isn't involved in sport may not understand that," Tessa says. "Whoever I end up with is going to have to understand that time commitment, and all that goes into being a competitive athlete. And leading

Above: (top) Scott kissing Tessa's cheek.
(Bottom) Attending the annual White Knight Gala, May 2010.

up to this point in our careers, ten hours at the rink every day at Canton, Michigan, doesn't give you much opportunity to meet people. Sure, we know everyone in the skating world for the most part, but if I'm looking for some sort of balance in my life, for something to complement the skating world, I just don't have the opportunity that most kids have to meet people. I'm not staying in a university dorm and able to go out on campus every night and mingle with my peers. I go to school, but I sit in the classroom for two classes,

then I'm heading to the gym to work out or I'm heading to the rink. It's a very different experience. I've become aware of that growing up, watching my older siblings go through university, meeting so many people or keeping the same friends from high school. Because we weren't at one high school, that hasn't happened. I'm not complaining, it's just a challenge."

Scott continues: "The other side of it, too, is that we play a couple when we are on the ice. When you have a man and a woman on the ice skating together, it makes sense that you play those roles. For Tessa and I that really works. You need to find people who understand that, and also know that when we're off the ice we make public appearances and we're working there as well. Off the ice we don't pretend that we're a couple, but a lot of our time is going into being together and working together. I don't think it's that much of a difference from a normal work relationship, but it is very time-consuming. That's where Tess and I have decided we're going to put our energy for as long as we're competitive skating. And you have to find someone who understands that, and I don't think it's as easy as it may sound."

While they still have an unspecified number of years left on the Olympic-eligible competitive scene, and professional tours will beckon when they do decide to abandon amateur competition, Tessa and Scott know that one day skating will end, no matter how much their legion of fans want it to continue forever. They'll remain the closest of friends, but their interests may take them in different directions. Scott prefers to concentrate on the here and now, which means competitive skating, but he's also given plenty of thought to the "'when' and 'what if' scenarios." He'll make sure he completes his education, "and I'd like to do something within sport in Canada. I don't know exactly what that might include; if it means working at Skate Canada, or Sport Canada, or the Canadian Olympic Committee, or even coaching and giving back to the sport. Patrice Lauzon and I have had talks about how it's a shame that so many top Canadian dance teams leave the country to train. Patrice has a great deal of passion for that idea. Canada has the best ice dancers in the world, so why don't we have that big training centre? There are some spots in the country where there are ice dance schools, and they do really good work. But our top teams have not trained in Canada since Tracy Wilson and Rob McCall, and that was in the mid-1980s. We love being in Michigan, but would we like to be in Canada? Yes."

There is a side of Tessa that is strongly drawn to the fashion industry, and she hopes to pursue some of the opportunities that Roots can provide her. "Anything involved in fashion would be amaz-

ing," she muses. "Obviously, it's a tough market, but even if it wasn't designing — if it was a position as a buyer or marketing, or whatever. But my dream is to go to school full-time. I'm on a long-term plan to graduate (from the University of Windsor) because I'm only going part-time. Ultimately, if I graduate with enough time, I would love to go to law school. It's not that I would necessarily like to practise law, but it's always been something I've had in the back of my mind. I would love the process and it would open a lot of doors, and it's really interesting. Right now it's a goal of mine, but so much can change before you get to that point."

The fluid ease with which they delivered their arduous Olympic programs was viewed by millions of people around the world, and prompted many lofty comparisons to past skating legends. Robin Cousins wasn't the only skating expert to refer to Jayne Torvill and Christopher Dean, regarded as the greatest ice dancers ever. And others compared their light touch, seamless programs, and childhood-born chemistry to two-time Olympic pairs champions Ekaterina Gordeeva and Sergei Grinkov. But it is always others making those comparisons, not Tessa and Scott.

"We're not presuming anything like that at all," Tessa says. "I'm not saying I don't want to be compared to people as great as them. At the end of this all it would be really nice if we weren't compared to anyone. If we were just remembered for being ourselves."

So how would Tessa Virtue and Scott Moir like to be remembered? What kind of legacy would they like to leave the sport?

Tessa speaks first.

"Better that people remember us as good people than as good skaters," she says. "But if we're talking about our legacy on the ice, it would be great if when people thought of us they thought, 'They were true dancers,' and that we made people feel something."

And Scott?

"I was just thinking about how awesome that was," he says, turning to his partner with admiration. 'We made people feel something.' I love that."

"AT THE END OF THIS ALL
IT WOULD BE REALLY NICE IF
WE WERE JUST REMEMBERED
FOR BEING OURSELVES." —*Tessa*

PHOTOGRAPHY CREDITS

Every reasonable effort has been made to trace ownership of copyright materials. The publisher will gladly rectify any inadvertent errors or omissions in credits in future editions.

CP IMAGES

Mike Ridewood, 16, 151, (top);

AP Photo/David Zalubowski, 86;

Andrew Vaughan, 87;

Paul Chiasson, 91, 105, 107, 108–109, 119, 123, 124–125, (centre), 142–143, (centre), 158, 159;

AP Photo/Lee Jin-Man, 92, 97, (top), 99;

AP Photo/Itsuo Inouye, 95;

AP Photo/Junji Jurokawa, 114, 126–127;

Darryl Dyck, 116, 120–121;

Mark Spowart, 138;

AP Photo/Ivan Sekretarev, 147;

Robert Skinner, 148;

AP Photo/Antonio Calanni, 178–179, (centre)

GETTY IMAGES

AFP Photo/Yuri Kadobnov, 5, 140, 141, 143, (bottom right);

Matthew Stockman, 6;

Kevork Djansezian, 13;

Chung Sung-Jun, 96;

Jamie McDonald, 100;

AFP Photo/Mark Ralston, 111;

AFP/Saeed Khan, 136–137;

Jasper Juinen, 144–145;

AFP/Dimitar Dilkoff, 150;

Clive Rose, 156–157;

NHLI via Getty Images/ Andre Ringuette, 166–167, (centre)

MYRA KLARMAN

2–3; 90; 102, (top right); 103; 170–171; 172; 173; 174–175; 186 (all photos)

ALMA MOIR

22, (all photos);	24;	31, (top left);	164, (centre left);
23, (all photos, bottom left photo c/o Cedar Lane Studios);	26 (bottom right); 27; 30;	97, (bottom right); 132, (bottom left); 152, (centre right);	164, (bottom); 177, (bottom right)

SUN MEDIA

129; 154, (bottom); 155; 163, (all photos); 164, (top); 165, (centre right)

KATE VIRTUE

19, (all photos);

20, (all photos);

25, (all photos);

26, (top left);

28, (all photos);

31, (centre right);

31, (bottom left);

32; 33; 36; 37; 38, (all photos);

39; 41, (all photos);

42; 43, (all photos);

44, (all photos);

45, (photo c/o Brian Dole);

46; 47; 48; 49, (all photos);

50; 51; 52–53, (all photos);

54, (all photos);

55; 58; 59; 60; 61, (all photos);

62, (photo c/o J. Barry Mittan);

63; 64–65; 66, (photo c/o Brian Dole);

67; 68, (all photos);

69, (all photos);

70; 72; 73, (all photos);

74; 75; 76, (all photos);

77; 78, (all photos, top right photo c/o Caroline Paré);

80, (all photos);

81; 84; 85; 88; 89; 93; 94; 98, (all photos);

101, (photo c/o *London Free Press*/Sue Reeve and Derek Ruttan/Sun Media);

102, (top left);

104;

106;

111, (top right);

118; 125, (top right);

130, (top left);

130–131 (centre);

132–133, (centre);

134; 135, (all photos);

149, (top);

149, (bottom right);

151, (bottom right);

152, (top);

152, (centre left);

152, (bottom);

153, (all photos);

154, (top);

168–169, (centre);

169, (all photos);

177, (centre);

178, (bottom left, photo c/o Mary McCain);

181;

189

Image on page 149 (bottom left) © Rick Madonik/GetStock.com

Image on page 162 © Stephan Potopnyk/*International Figure Skating* magazine

Image on page 166 (top left) © Cylla Von Tiedemann

Image on page 166 (bottom left) © Sport Korea

ACKNOWLEDGEMENTS

Thank you to our fabulous, loving families who have not only provided unconditional love and support, but also sacrificed immensely and encouraged us to go after our dreams. You've kept us grounded and served as our perfect "safe place" throughout this rollercoaster of a journey.

To those Canadian ice dancers that came before us — Tracy Wilson and Rob McCall, Shae-Lynn Bourne and Victor Kraatz, Megan Wing and Aaron Lowe, and Marie-France Dubreuil and Patrice Lauzon — thank you for paving the way. Your creativity, work ethic, and class were inspirational. Thanks for showing us that anything is possible.

Our journey started at the Ilderton Skating Club and has included a magnificent cast of professionals who helped launch our career. Thanks so much to Carol Moir, Paul MacIntosh, Suzanne Killing-Wood, and Rebecca Babb, who gave us excellent basic skating skills and shaped our approach to training, competing, and relating to one another. They taught us many lessons that reach far beyond the boards of a rink and made us strive to be the "class of the ice."

To Marina Zoueva, Igor Shpilband, and Johnny Johns for their vision, dedication, focus, and unwavering faith in our skills. Thank you for never giving up and for sharing your expertise so thoughtfully. You provided us with the material that made us remember why we love what we do. Thank you for encouraging us to skate from the heart. You are more than our coaches — you are family.

To our wonderful "dream team" support staff who keep our bodies in top shape: Mary Brannagan, Maria Mountain, Brian Gastaldi, Earl Wenk, John Vickers, Dr. Randy Tent, Dr. Michael Ware, and the staff at Poise Pilates. Thank you for being the reason we are able to do what we love to do and feel our best.

Thanks to Skate Canada for providing us with opportunities and experiences that reached a pinnacle at a home Olympic Games. You gave us the tools and resources that ultimately helped us in handling the pressure of competition. Special thanks to Marilyn Chidlow, Anne Shaw, David Dore, Benoît Lavoie, Marijane Stong, and Louis Stong for their encouragement, direction, and advice — much love and hugs.

Thank you to Gillian and Paul Baay. From a business deal to an incredible friendship — we love you both. Your support is invaluable.

Of course, we have to mention our enormous appreciation for help from Own the Podium, the Canadian Olympic Committee, Sport Canada, and B2ten without whose financial assistance we would not have been able to continue skating!

A heartfelt thanks to Steve Milton, for whom we have the utmost respect, and who helped us tell our story and made the process most enjoyable.

Enormous and sincere thanks to David Pelletier for helping us deal with the pressures leading up to and surrounding the Olympics, as well as handling our transition into the business world. Your time, generosity, and guidance have been pivotal to our success!

And a huge thank you to our loyal fans who continually amaze and motivate us! Your support and cheers never go unnoticed.

— *Tessa and Scott*

To my inner circle, Jess, Toby, Michelle, Mom, with deep thanks for your support. To Tessa and Scott for being the great skaters, but more importantly, the great people that they are. And to Kelly, Janie, Sarah, and everyone else at House of Anansi Press for the encouragement and belief.

—*Steve Milton*

ABOUT THE AUTHORS

TESSA VIRTUE and SCOTT MOIR won the 2010 Olympic gold medal in ice dancing. They are also the 2010 World champions, the 2008 Four Continents champions, the 2006 World Junior champions, and the 2008–2010 Canadian National champions. They received the first perfect score for ice dancing under the International Skating Union (ISU) Judging System, and are the current world record score holders for the Original Dance. As of August 2010, they are ranked third in the world by the ISU.

STEVE MILTON is a columnist for the *Hamilton Spectator* who has covered six Winter Olympics and more than twenty World Figure Skating Championships. He is the author of twelve figure skating books, including *Figure Skating's Greatest Stars* and *Figure Skating Now*.

TESSA&
SCOTT

House of Anansi Press Inc.
110 Spadina Avenue, Suite 801, Toronto, ON, M5V 2K4